The

Newbery

and

Caldecott

Awards

▶ A Guide
to the
Medal
and
Honor
Books

2004
Edition

Association for
Library Service to Children

AMERICAN LIBRARY ASSOCIATION
Chicago   2004

The Newbery and Caldecott medals and Honor Book seals are property of the American Library Association and cannot be used in any form or reproduced without permission of the ALA, Office of Rights and Permissions.

Photo of Mordicai Gerstein courtesy of Stephen Petegorsky. Cover illustration of *The Man Who Walked between the Towers* used with permission of the publisher.

Cover illustration of *The Tale of Despereaux: Being the Story of a Mouse, a Princess, Some Soup, and a Spool of Thread* by Timothy Basil Ering used with permission of the publisher.

The paper used in this publication meets the minimum requirements of American National Standard for Information Sciences—Permanence of Paper for Printed Library Materials, ANSI Z39.48-1992.∞

ISBN 0-8389-3542-7

ISSN 1070-4493

Printed in the United States of America.

08 07 06 05 04   5 4 3 2 1

CONTENTS

PREFACE   v

Newbery and Caldecott Awards:
   Authorization and Terms   1

Reading Pictures: Searching for Excellence
   in Picture Books
      Gratia J. Banta   9

The Newbery Awards, 2004–1922   19

The Caldecott Awards, 2004–1938   87

The Media Used in Caldecott Picture Books:
   Notes toward a Definitive List   139

AUTHOR/ILLUSTRATOR INDEX   163
TITLE INDEX   170

PREFACE

Welcome to the 2004 edition of the Newbery and Caldecott Awards guide. The Newbery and Caldecott medal and honor books represent the best of the best in children's book publishing. This book offers librarians, teachers, educators, parents, and children more than 80 years of exemplary literature to share and enjoy. Its rich collection of award-winning titles provides librarians and educators with core lists for library collection and curricula development, readers' advisory, and quick reference.

In this year's essay, "Reading Pictures: Searching for Excellence in Picture Books," Gratia J. Banta, an artist and former children's librarian, discusses how we can teach ourselves to recognize distinguished book illustrations. Banta outlines a host of necessary elements, such as visual literacy and knowledge of art history, art terms, and techniques, which can help prepare professionals to search for and identify excellence in picture book illustration.

Bette J. Peltola's essay "Newbery and Caldecott Awards: Authorization and Terms" discusses the terms and definitions that have evolved for both medals. She provides insight into the significance of the awards and into the evaluation of children's literature.

Descriptive annotations provide a brief summary of each medal and honor book named since the inception of each award. "Media Used in Caldecott Picture Books" reveals each illustrator's choice of media for the medal and honor books (1938–2004) and includes a helpful glossary of art terms. For the 2004 winners, we have also included photos of the medalists and the remarks of the award committee chairs, taken from the press announcements, to help capture some of the enthusiasm and excitement that accompany the selection and presentation of the awards.

While we know you will find the 2004 guide useful, we also encourage your suggestions for future editions.

MALORE I. BROWN
Executive Director
Association for Library Service to Children

Newbery and Caldecott Awards
Authorization and Terms

BETTE J. PELTOLA

Each year the Newbery and Caldecott Medals are awarded by the American Library Association for the most distinguished American children's books published the previous year. On June 21, 1921, Frederic G. Melcher proposed to the American Library Association meeting of the Children's Librarians' Section that a medal be given for the most distinguished children's book of the year. He suggested that it be named for the eighteenth-century English bookseller John Newbery. The idea was enthusiastically accepted by the children's librarians, and Melcher's official proposal was approved by the ALA Executive Board in 1922. In Melcher's formal agreement with the board, the purpose of the Newbery Medal was stated as follows: "To encourage original and creative work in the field of books for children. To emphasize to the public that contributions to the literature for children deserve similar recognition to poetry, plays, or novels. To give those librarians, who make it their life work to serve children's reading interests, an opportunity to encourage good writing in this field." The Newbery Award thus became the first children's book award in the world. Its terms, as well as its long history, continue to make it the best known and most discussed children's book award in this country.

The description of the award adopted in 1922 indicated that the Newbery Medal "is to be awarded annually to the author of the 'most distinguished contribution to American literature for children,' the award being made to cover books whose publication in book form falls in the calendar year last elapsed. The award is restricted to authors who are citizens or residents of the United States. Reprints and compilations

BETTE J. PELTOLA is professor emerita, School of Education, University of Wisconsin–Milwaukee.

are not eligible for consideration. There are no limitations as to the character of the book considered except that it be original work. It need not be written solely for children; the judgment of the librarians voting shall decide whether a book be a 'contribution to the literature for children.' The award considers only the books of one calendar year and does not pass judgment on the author's previous work or other work during that year outside the volume that may be named." In 1932 the Section for Library Work with Children, with Melcher's approval, adopted the following: "To be eligible for the Newbery Medal books must be original, or, if traditional in origin, the result of individual research, the retelling and reinterpretation being the writer's own."

During the next several years, many persons became concerned that the artists creating picture books for children were as deserving of honor and encouragement as were the authors of children's books. So, in 1937 Melcher suggested a second annual medal, this to be given to the artist who had created the most distinguished picture book of the year and to be called the Caldecott Medal in honor of Randolph Caldecott, the nineteenth-century English illustrator. The idea for this medal was also accepted enthusiastically by the Section for Library Work with Children of ALA and was approved by the ALA Executive Board.

The Caldecott Medal "shall be awarded to the artist of the most distinguished American Picture Book for Children published in the United States during the preceding year. The award shall go to the artist, who must be a citizen or resident of the United States, whether or not he be the author of the text. Members of the Newbery Medal Committee will serve as judges. If a book of the year is nominated for both the Newbery and Caldecott Awards the committee shall decide under which heading it shall be voted upon, so that the same title shall not be considered on both ballots." In 1977 the Board of Directors of the Association for Library Service to Children rescinded the final part of the 1937 action and approved that "any book published in the preceding year shall be eligible to be considered for either award or both awards." Separate committees to choose the Newbery and Caldecott Awards were established in 1978 and began with the 1980 Selection Committees.

ADDITIONAL CHANGES IN TERMS FOR THE AWARDS

A resolution by the Section for Library Work with Children in 1932 that "the book of a previous award winner shall receive the award only upon the unanimous vote" of the committee was later rescinded by the Children's Services Division Board of Directors. "In view of the fact that a unanimous vote in the case of a previous winner of the Newbery or Caldecott Awards was first instituted to encourage new authors and illustrators at a period when such encouragement was needed and since such need is no longer apparent, the restriction of a unanimous vote for winning either award more than once [is] removed from terms for selection [of the awards]" (1958). In 1963 it was voted by the Children's Services Division that "joint authors shall be eligible" for the awards.

In 1978, the ALSC Board of Directors adopted new statements of terms, definitions, and criteria for each award. The new statements were prepared and adopted to provide further clarification of the basis on which the awards are to be given. They were slightly modified for further clarification in 1985 and 1987.

NEWBERY AWARD

The terms, definitions, and criteria for the Newbery Award are as follows:

TERMS

1. The Medal shall be awarded annually to the author of the most distinguished contribution to American literature for children published in the United States during the preceding year. There are no limitations as to the character of the book considered except that it be original work. Honor Books may be named. These shall be books that are also truly distinguished.

2. The Award is restricted to authors who are citizens or residents of the United States.

3. The committee in its deliberations is to consider only the books eligible for the Award as specified in the terms.

DEFINITIONS

1. "*Contribution* to American *literature*" indicates the text of a book. It also implies that the committee shall consider all forms of writing—fiction, nonfiction, and poetry. Reprints and compilations are not eligible.

2. A "Contribution to American literature for *children*" shall be a book for which children are a potential audience. The book displays respect for children's understandings, abilities, and appreciations. "Children" are defined as persons of ages up to and including fourteen, and books for this entire age range are to be considered.

3. "Distinguished" is defined as:
   - marked by eminence and distinction: noted for significant achievement
   - marked by excellence in quality
   - marked by conspicuous excellence or eminence
   - individually distinct

4. "Author" may include coauthors. The author may be awarded the medal posthumously.

5. In defining the term "original work," the committee will consider books that are traditional in origin if the book is the result of original research and the retelling and interpretation are the writer's own.

6. "American literature published in the United States" means that books originally published in other countries are not eligible.

7. "Published . . . during the preceding year" means that the book has a publication date in that year, was available for purchase in that year, and has a copyright date no later than that year. A book might have a copyright date prior to the year under consideration but, for various reasons, was not published until the year under consideration.

8. "Resident" specifies that the author has established and maintained residence in the United States as distinct from being a casual or occasional visitor.

9. The term "only the books eligible for the Award" specifies that the committee is not to consider the entire body of the work of an author or whether the author has previously won the award. The committee's decision is to be made following deliberations about the books of the specified calendar year.

CRITERIA

1. In identifying distinguished writing in a book for children:
   a. Committee members need to consider:
      Interpretation of the theme or concept.

      Presentation of information including accuracy, clarity, and organization.

      Development of plot.

      Delineation of characters.

      Delineation of setting.

      Appropriateness of style.

   Note: Because the literary qualities to be considered will vary depending on content, the committee need not expect to find excellence in each of the named elements. The book should, however, have distinguished qualities in all of the elements pertinent to it.

   b. Committee members must consider excellence of presentation for a child audience.

2. Each book is to be considered as a contribution to literature. The committee is to make its decision primarily on the text. Other aspects of a book are to be considered only if they distract from the text. Such other aspects might include illustrations, overall design of the book, etc.

   Note: The committee should keep in mind that the award is for literary quality and quality of presentation for children. The award is not for didactic intent or for popularity.

CALDECOTT AWARD

The terms, definitions, and criteria for the Caldecott Award are as follows:

TERMS

1. The Medal shall be awarded annually to the artist of the most distinguished American picture book for children published in the United States during the preceding year. There are no limitations as to the character of the picture book except that the illustrations be original work. Honor Books may be named. These shall be books that are also truly distinguished.

2. The Award is restricted to artists who are citizens or residents of the United States.

3. The committee in its deliberations is to consider only the books eligible for the Award, as specified in the terms.

DEFINITIONS

1. A "picture book for children," as distinguished from other books with illustrations, is one that essentially provides the child with a visual experience. A picture book has a collective unity of story-line, theme, or concept, developed through the series of pictures of which the book is comprised.

2. A "picture book for children" is one for which children are a potential audience. The book displays respect for children's understandings, abilities, and appreciations. "Children" are defined as persons of ages up to and including fourteen, and picture books for this entire age range are to be considered.

3. "Distinguished" is defined as:
   - marked by eminence and distinction: noted for significant achievement
   - marked by excellence in quality
   - marked by conspicuous excellence or eminence
   - individually distinct

4. The "artist" is the illustrator or co-illustrators. The artist may be awarded the Medal posthumously.

5. "Original work" means that illustrations reprinted or compiled from other sources are not eligible.

6. "American picture book published in the United States" specifies that books originally published in other countries are not eligible.

7. "Published . . . in the preceding year" means that the book has a publication date in that year, was available for purchase in that year, and has a copyright date no later than that year. A book might have a copyright date prior to the year under consideration but, for various reasons, was not published until the year under consideration.

8. "Resident" specifies that the artist has established and maintained residence in the United States as distinct from being a casual or occasional visitor.

9. The term "only the books eligible for the Award" specifies that the committee is not to consider the entire body of the work by an artist or whether the artist has previously won the award. The committee's decision is to be made following deliberation about the picture books of the specified calendar year.

CRITERIA

1. In identifying a distinguished picture book for children:
    a. Committee members need to consider:

    Excellence of execution in the artistic technique employed.

    Excellence of pictorial interpretation of story, theme, or concept; of appropriateness of style of illustration to the story, theme, or concept; of delineation of plot, theme, characters, setting, mood, or information through the pictures.

    b. Committee members must consider excellence of presentation in recognition of a child audience.
2. The only limitation to graphic form is that the form must be one which may be used in a picture book (e.g., motion-picture photography is not at present possible, though still photography is).
3. Each book is to be considered as a picture book. The committee is to make its decision primarily on the illustrations, but other components of a book are to be considered especially when they make a book less effective as a children's picture book. Such other components might include the written text, the overall design of the book, etc.

    Note: The committee should keep in mind that the award is for distinguished illustrations in a picture book and for excellence of pictorial presentation for children. The award is not for didactic intent or for popularity.

AWARD COMMITTEES

The committees that select the Newbery and the Caldecott Medal and Honor Books each have fifteen members including the chair. The ALSC membership elects the chair and seven members from a slate drawn up by the nominating committee; the ALSC president-elect appoints the remaining seven members. All members of the committees are members of ALSC.

During the year, each committee member reads as many of the eligible books as possible, including all books suggested by other committee members and by other members of ALSC. Twice in the autumn, committee members cast preliminary ballots to begin to focus attention on the books likely to be of most interest in the selection discussions. No eligible book which has been suggested before the midwinter selection meetings is excluded from consideration, however, even if it was not nominated on a preliminary ballot. During the selection meetings, the committee discusses all nominated and suggested books before beginning balloting. Each committee member votes for three books, with four points assigned to first choice, three to second, and two to third choice. To win, a book must receive at least eight first place choices and at least eight points more than any other book. Once a winner is chosen, the committee decides whether to name honor books and how many.

DESCRIPTION OF THE MEDALS

In 1921 Melcher had the Newbery Medal designed by René Paul Chambellan. In 1937 Chambellan designed the Caldecott Medal. The bronze medals, shown on page 8, have the winner's name and the date engraved on the back. The ALA Executive Board in 1922 delegated to the Children's Librarians' Section the responsibility for selecting the book to receive the Newbery Medal. The inscription on the Newbery Medal still reads "Children's Librarians' Section," although the section has changed its name four times and its membership now includes both school and public library children's librarians in contrast to the years 1922–58, when the section, under three different names, included only public library children's librarians. (The section names: until 1929, Children's Librarians' Section; 1929–42, Section for Library Work with Children; 1942–58, Children's Library Association; 1958–77, Children's Service Division; and, Association for Library Service to Children (ALSC), 1977 to date.)

When the Caldecott Medal was accepted in 1937, the Section for Library Work with Children invited the School Libraries Section (now American Association of School Librarians) to name five of its members to the awards committee each year. For this reason the Caldecott Medal inscription reads: "Awarded annually by the Children's and School Librarians Sections of the American Library Association." This is a combination and simplification of the actual names of the sections. The wording continues even though several ALA reorganizations resulted in 1958 in the present divisions, among them the Children's Services Division (now the Association for Library Service to Children), made up of public library children's librarians, school librarians, and others interested in children's library services and good books for children. In 1958 the Children's Services Division Board of Directors recognized that the wording on both medals was incorrect in terms of current ALA terminology. It realized that confusion about the membership of the committee that chooses the medal winners could result from the discrepancies. However, the CSD board decided to request no change in the inscription on either medal, preferring to have them continue in their original form and design. Responsibility for both awards resides with ALSC, formerly the CSD.

HONOR BOOKS

From the beginning of the awarding of the medals, committees could, and usually did, cite other books as worthy of attention. Such books were referred to as runners-up. In 1971 the term "runners-up," used to designate books cited with the annual Newbery and Caldecott Medal winners, was changed to "honor books." The new terminology was made retroactive so that all runners-up are now referred to as Newbery or Caldecott Honor Books.

At the same meeting, the Board of Directors of the Children's Services Division approved silver facsimile seals with the designation "Newbery Honor Book" and "Caldecott Honor Book," which may be placed on the honor books in similar fashion to the use made of the gold facsimile seals of the medals placed on the award-winning books. The gold and silver facsimile seals are sold by the Association for Library Service to Children, with all profits going to support the division's programs, including the Frederic G. Melcher Scholarship Fund. Permission for photographic reproduction of the medals is also controlled by the association; profits from commercial reproduction also go to the Scholarship Fund.

In 1978 the ALSC board approved the presentation of certificates to the authors of the Newbery Honor Books and the illustrators of the Caldecott Honor Books. Certificates were presented for the first time in 1986.

Although some procedures have changed over the years the awards have been given, and some rules or aspects of what the awards are for have been clarified or modified, the basic purpose of honoring distinguished American children's books has not changed. Numerous committees have studied virtually every aspect of the award-giving procedure, the rationale, and the impact of the awards over the years. Such study is likely to continue and ensures a vital life to these awards that have had such an impact on the quality of American literature for children.

JOHN NEWBERY MEDAL	THE CALDECOTT MEDAL

Reading Pictures
Searching for Excellence in Picture Books

GRATIA J. BANTA

First there were cave drawings, then illuminated manuscripts and large paintings telling religious stories. Indian pictographs gave directions. My grandmother told me she used chalk to make drawings on the outside walls of her home to tell hoboes she had extra milk for them. Throughout history, pictures have been used to tell stories that change people's lives. All of these visual images were ways to communicate to others without words.

Research shows that visual skills precede verbal skills. Very young children learn to read pictures well before they learn to read text. It has always been easy for me to read pictures. When my mother read to me, before I could read, I memorized each subtle nuance of the pen-and-ink sketches by Ernest H. Shepard that illustrate A. A. Milne's *When We Were Very Young* and *Now We Are Six*. I know I did this because when I look at those sketches today they are like old friends. They reassured me that all of my feelings were valid. Elizabeth Ann in the poem "Explained" has a question about God, and "she would run round the world till she found" the answer. Shepard draws Elizabeth, her head held high, her hair flying, her body in a spirited run, and her fists full of determination. The rabbits sitting by the side of the road and watching Elizabeth can see that she has a question and that it matters very much to her. I read the sketch to mean that a young girl could go on an adventure. I have treasured that image, and my young heart's belief in it, for my entire life. Christopher Robin in "Sneezles" sits patiently in bed with a cold, and I can see that drawing clearly when I have to rest in bed, and it comforts me.

GRATIA J. BANTA served as a children's librarian for more than twenty years. She currently devotes her time to painting and teaching visual literacy in nationally recognized workshops. She served on the 1988 Caldecott Committee and has been an ALSC member for eighteen years. See: www.gratiaarts.com

In the first grade, when I was taught to read using the Dick and Jane series, I was encouraged again to read the pictures. I was not alone. By the 1950s, 80 percent of the first graders in the United States were learning to read by the whole-word method instead of by phonetically sounding out words letter by letter. We were asked to think about the activities taking place in the pictures and to discuss them in class. The colorful illustrations by Eleanor Campbell were based on photos of real children doing real activities. Over time it is estimated that over eighty-five million children learned to read that way. Whether they are called decorations, as they were in *Now We Are Six* when it was first published in 1927, illustrations, or paintings, as they are sometimes called in picture books today, they form the visual stories that continue to challenge, enlighten, excite, and satisfy me.

From 1976 to 2001, as a professional children's librarian, I had the opportunity to share new picture books weekly with children. During that time children's book publishing enjoyed an explosion of creative changes in format and printing along with huge increases in sales and number of titles. In 1969 Eric Carle's *The Very Hungry Caterpillar* offered a then-radical format with cutout holes representing where the caterpillar had eaten. In the 1980s Paul Zelinsky's spectacular pop-up songbook *The Wheels on the Bus* was so well loved that my library could not buy enough copies to keep one on the shelf.

Working in rural libraries, I quickly found that book illustration could be used not only as an introduction to reading but also as an introduction to exploring the larger world of the fine arts. While serving on the 1988 Caldecott Committee, I learned that my lifelong love of reading the pictures would help steer other committee members and myself to identify excellence in picture books while selecting "the most distinguished American picture book for children."

By learning to read the pictures, we librarians, parents, and teachers can

> Learn about cultures outside our communities
>
> Excite our visual senses and challenge our visual literacy
>
> Educate the eye and put illustration in the context of all arts
>
> Increase our enjoyment of the world as a visual place
>
> Share a book on a visual level and thus include reluctant readers and visual learners
>
> Enjoy a book with a preliterate child
>
> Understand and respect the skills and career of an illustrator
>
> Extend the role of the arts in our communities
>
> Expand the meaning of the written word
>
> Identify excellence in book design

The best, most rewarding reason is contained in the Indian word *rasa,* which is the moment of heightened awareness achieved when we perceive the ultimate reality of a work of art. It happens to the viewer of the art. (A different delight occurs in the making of the art.) It is like the magical blooming of a flower, a flash of light, an insight, the delight in learning, the sense of wonderment, the sense of the miracle of ourselves. For those of us who love looking at art, *rasa* is the reason we keep coming back for more. It is also the reason that we search for excellence in painting and illustration. Once viewers experience *rasa,* they will no longer settle for inferior work. Young and old search for *rasa* in the visual world and know and cherish its feeling of joy.

By reading pictures with an educated eye, a sense of their intended audience, and a heart open to the feelings they evoke, we can begin our search for excellence in picture books. We can then share our findings by acknowledging the most brilliantly illustrated books in our reviews, our selections, and our awards. While serving on the Caldecott Committee, I was asked to address adults about excellence in picture book illustration, so I developed a workshop called "Reading the Pictures."

We librarians can train ourselves, as adults, to think in pictures again. Such thinking is called visual literacy. Developing visual literacy is much the same as learning a foreign language. I invite you to open a picture book as if you were a child not yet able to read. Ignore the words and look only at the pictures. This is the first step that needs to be taken to identify exceptional book illustration. Second, read the text but continue to notice the illustrations. Third, read both text and illustrations together, taking time to reflect and set aside any adult filters.

When we have learned to read the pictures, we can each find our own voice to describe our personal reactions. The goal is to determine if the illustrations and the book meet the high standard of being distinguished and exceptional. We owe it to the book industry and especially to book illustrators to get beyond describing illustrations as "pretty" or "interesting" and to choose our words carefully. As Picasso once said, "If you must insult me, at least get your terminology straight!"

How then can we best prepare to identify the most distinguished picture books? I recommend the following:

> Learn the elements of composition and design.
>
> Understand cultural context and color.
>
> Determine whether the text has been enhanced or extended by the illustrations.
>
> Learn how to link book illustration with the other fine arts.
>
> Recognize excellence in techniques used in a wide variety of materials.
>
> Identify which materials work well with a text.
>
> Identify excellence in bookmaking.
>
> Develop a working knowledge of art terms.
>
> Cultivate a basic knowledge of art history.
>
> Know the history of book illustration.
>
> Look at the original art of book illustrators.
>
> Listen to book illustrators and read what they say about their own work.
>
> Allow yourself time to do some of your own drawing or painting.

To illustrate the elements of composition and design, we will compare *Patience,* a painting by Balthus (see http://home.uchicago.edu/~susannah/patience.jpg), to the illustration in *Bunny Cakes,* by Rosemary Wells (Dial Books, 1997), above the text "This time Max wrote 'Red-Hot Marshmallow Squirters' in the most beautiful writing he knew." In the painting by Balthus we see a young woman bent forward to read a book that is opened flat and lying on a table. In the Wells illustration we see Max, a rabbit wearing a green striped jumpsuit with a purple T-shirt, leaning forward and scribbling on a lined yellow sheet of paper. In the design of each of their bending bodies, we feel a certain discomfort. In the painting by Balthus, it is about the sensual strength of a pubescent teenager. In the illustration by Wells, because Max cannot write, he is struggling to draw a picture to explain what he needs. There is no unused space in either image; even the blank white space around Max's frame and the dark curtain near the girl matter. Both figures fill the frame, and they seem to be exploding out of their boxes. The figures are full of passion and energy, and their compositions suggest that they are on the verge of being changed forever. Both works are successful because they clearly tell us about the emotional states of their characters, and we are filled with the energy of those characters' youth and a sense of their longing.

To better understand how color reflects a cultural context, see the contemporary work of Xenobia Bailey at http://www.uwrf.edu/history/prints/afr-amer/xenobia-bailey.html, and compare it to the illustrations in *Tar Beach,* by Faith Ringgold (Crown, 1991). Textile artists like Bailey use the bright colors of Africa. Similar colors are used in *Tar Beach,* a Caldecott Honor Book, representing a celebration of African heritage. In the 1980s Faith Ringgold used acrylic on canvas to make paintings of quilts that told about her life. *The Purple Quilt* (http://www.faithringgold.com/ringgold/d02.htm) is an example. When Ringgold turned to illustration, her sense of color became a cultural experience for all to enjoy. She asked us to take her primitive, or naive, art seriously, as if to say, "This may not be familiar to you, but it's all about my culture, my family, my heritage, and my life as an artist," and offering a lesson in understanding cultural context.

Illustrators employ many strategies in their effort to extend text. Words are few in *Tuesday* by David Wiesner (Clarion, 1991). The entire text, spread over thirty-two pages, consists of "TUESDAY EVENING AROUND EIGHT," "11:21 PM," "4:38 AM" and "NEXT TUESDAY, 7:58 PM." Economy of words forces the reader not to depend on the text for the story. This is first of all a visual story. The watercolor images are realistic, but their actions are not. Life is not what it seems, and we are the aliens. The ending picture features flying pigs. Is Wiesner referring to the phrase "when pigs fly," asking us to suspend disbelief? Such mysterious questions extend the text and add to the excitement of the book. Years later, we can look back and say those flying pigs foreshadowed Wiesner's *The Three Pigs* (Clarion, 2001).

Perhaps illustrators who extend the text draw on the work of Randolph Caldecott. In his illustrations for *Hey Diddle Diddle* (George Routledge and Sons, 1882), the pigs seem to be wearing suits and dancing to music, giving us more to enjoy about the pigs than the text provides. On another page, Caldecott draws the moon so low on the horizon that a cow need not jump far for us to believe the rhyme. "Look how the cow jumps over the moon! I wish I had such a clever mind!" exclaimed another brilliant and successful British illustrator, Kate Greenaway, a contemporary and a good friend of Caldecott. The illustrator Maurice Sendak writes about this illustration, noting the additional figure in the frame. "It's Caldecott's drawing of the milkmaid dropping her bucket that makes this even more exceptional, as in her reaction we learn that she sees what we see also." Again, Caldecott extends and enhances the text, in this case giving credibility to the rhyme. (For more, read Maurice Sendak, *Caldecott and Co.: Notes on Books and Pictures* [Farrar, 1988], and Ina Taylor, *The Art of Kate Greenaway: A Nostalgic Portrait of Childhood* [Pelican, 1991]).

Picture books can serve as a bridge to other arts. Film is a close cousin to picture books. In film and picture books, the images and scenes are repeated to carry out a story. A distinction between the media needs to be made. Films, like picture books, are composed of a series of images that form a story by following the same characters through a variety of settings in which the story unfolds. For example, all of the frogs that Wiesner paints remain the same kind of frogs, page after page. A painting does not require this sequence. Except in some narrative paintings, a painting is not about the development of characters over time. In Wiesner's *Tuesday,* we sense we are in a colorful science fiction film. Wiesner's frogs are painted in a realistic style; they are not painted from the imagination. But when he paints them flying on lily pads, it defies our scientific knowledge, which gives us the sense of being in a science fiction film.

As we learn more about book illustration, we will find sometimes subtle, sometimes direct references to the great artists. Anthony Browne made references to paintings in *Willy the Dreamer* (Candlewick Press, 1997). Browne informs audiences that the painter Magritte is an influence and that he admires the writing of Lewis Carroll, so it is no surprise that we can find connections to Magritte and Carroll throughout Browne's work. In the second edition of *Willy's Pictures* (Candlewick Press, 2000), the referenced paintings are reproduced at the end of the book.

Some books are about music. *Mysterious Thelonious,* written by Christopher Raschka (Orchard Books, 1997) and dedicated to the editor Dick Jackson, is just such a book. Its dust jacket, with grid pattern and musical scale, sets the stage, and I can hear the instruments getting tuned up. The text is spread across several pages. The words "Oh so mysterious Thelonious, mysterious Thelonious, mysterious Thelonious, mysterious, oh so" can be found swimming through Raschka's fluid, floating musical scale. The placement of the text is a sensuous feast for the eye. We are told on the end pages that Raschka "matched the twelve musical tones of the chromatic scale, e.g., do, re, mi, to the twelve color values of the color wheel, then set paint strokes for notes and color washes for harmonies." It looks and feels like the music of Monk translated into colorful watercolor. The book measures only 6½ inches by 7 ½ inches, inviting small children to hold it and enjoy the colors, and perhaps to hear their own personal rendition of the music referenced and to know about its message before ever listening to Monk's "Mysterioso."

Bridging from book illustration to poetry, Angela Johnson was inspired by *Tar Beach* and wrote this poem.

> When it is a warm time
> in the evening
> and my people are
>   laughing
> and warm
> beside me,
> it almost feels like
> I can fly.
> Above the city and
>   everything
> I know.
> —And I am happy in
>   the coolness
> as I am in the warmth,
> because I can fly as
> free as I feel
> and watch my people
> with love
> from
> above.

More examples of poems inspired by art appear in Jan Greenberg's *Heart to Heart: New Poems Inspired by Twentieth-Century American Art* (Abrams, 2001).

To further our understanding of visual literacy, museums offer the most excellent examples of a wide variety of materials and techniques used by artists. Labels and exhibit catalogs provide more information. To develop a critical and educated eye takes some work over time. As you learn to recognize the variety of materials used, you might work in reverse and imagine what stories they would complement. For example, the quilts Faith Ringgold painted would work well in a story about an African American girl growing up in Harlem. In this way you will be able to determine whether a certain medium works well with a text. Go to "images" at http://www.google.com to search for paintings and illustrations.

To identify excellence in bookmaking, the binding, layout, design, and overall look of a book must be considered. To learn the terms that describe the parts of a book, read *ABC for Book Collectors*, 8th edition, by John Carter and Nicolas Barker (Oak Knoll Press, 2003). View early printed books on display in rare book collections. Examine books made by artists. They help us see books as art objects and demonstrate the creative use of experimental papers and bindings. Helpful websites include Minnesota Center for Book Arts, http://www.mnbookarts.org; the Center for Book Arts, http://www.centerforbookarts.org; and the San Francisco Center for the Book, http://www.sfcb.org/index.php3.

Once you have developed a working knowledge of art terms, you can more deeply appreciate picture books and more enthusiastically share them with children. If you can write book reviews that include knowledgeable comments about illustration, you will help publishers, authors, and illustrators. Illustrators and art directors read children's book reviews and can quickly spot a charlatan. And they know that starred reviews and awards result in stronger sales. There is, therefore, a great need for responsibility in writing reviews.

Unfortunately, many good books about illustration are out of print, but you can find them at the library. Sources for information about illustration are: *Art and Design in Children's Picture Books: An Analysis of Caldecott Award-Winning Illustrations,* by Lyn Ellen Lacy (American Library Association, 1986); *Looking at Picture Books,* by John Warren Stewig (Highsmith, 1995); *Lotus Seeds: Children, Pictures, and Books,* by Marcia Brown (Atheneum, 1986); *Potential of Picture Books: From Visual Literacy to Aesthetic Understanding,* by Barbara Z. Kiefer (Merrill/Prentice Hall, 1995); *Writing with Pictures: How to Write and Illustrate Children's Books,* by Uri Shulevitz (Watson-Guptill, 1997); *Picture This: How Pictures Work,* by Molly Garrett Bang (Seastar, 2000); and *Ways of Telling: Conversations on the Art of the Picture Book,* by Leonard S. Marcus (Dutton, 2002).

Information about art materials and techniques can be found in the *Artist's Handbook of Materials and Techniques,* by Ralph Mayer (Viking, 1991), *The Painters Handbook,* by David Gottsegen (Watson-Guptill, 1993), *The Oxford Dictionary of Art,* edited by Ian Chilvers and Harold Osborne (Oxford University Press, 1988), and, for more serious study, *Secret Knowledge: Rediscovering the Lost Techniques of the Old Masters* by David Hockney (Viking, 2001). It is also helpful to read journals that focus on the communication arts, such as *Print: America's Graphic Design Magazine* and the basic art journals.

To cultivate a basic knowledge of art history, read H. W. Janson and Anthony F. Janson, *History of Art for Young People,* sixth edition (Abrams, 2003). Enjoy Sister Wendy Beckett's *The Story of Painting* (DK Publishing, 1994) in book form or on video. Study *American Visions: The Epic History of Art in America,* by Robert Hughes (Knopf, 1997). View videos about individual artists such as Jackson Pollock and Frida Kahlo. Attend lectures on art history. Read children's biographies, such as Ann Kay Beneduce's *A Weekend with Winslow Homer* (Rizzoli, 1996), John Duggleby's *Story Painter: The Life of Jacob Lawrence* (Chronicle Books, 1998), Russell Freedman's *Martha Graham: A Dancer's Life* (Clarion, 1998), Paolo Guarnieri's *A Boy Named Giotto* (Farrar, 1999), Sandra Jordan and Jan Greenberg's *Frank O. Gehry: Outside In* (DK Publishing, 2000), Bijon LeTord's *A Bird or Two: A Story about Henri Matisse* (Eerdmans, 1999), Elizabeth Partridge's *Restless Spirit: The Life and Work of Dorothea Lange* (Viking,1998), Deborah Kogan Ray's *Hokusai: The Man Who Painted a Mountain* (Farrar, 2001), and Diane Stanley's *Michelangelo* (Harper Collins, 2000). Three children's fiction titles that feature artists are Janet Taylor

Lisle's *The Art of Keeping Cool* (Simon and Schuster, 2000), Linda Sue Park's *A Single Shard* (Clarion, 2001), and Gloria Whelan's *Homeless Bird* (HarperCollins, 2000).

Book illustration has a rich and global history, from illuminated manuscripts to lift-the-flap books to laser printing. As your knowledge expands, you'll want to learn about other awards for illustration, such as the Hans Christian Andersen Award, the Kate Greenaway Medal, and the various Bologna international book awards. Each of us is connected with some piece of that history. For me it is the teacher's guides for my first readers, the Dick and Jane series, which encouraged students to talk about the pictures in class. Reading experts Zerna Sharp and William Gray and an editorial team including May Hill Arbuthnot created a curriculum of reading books that reflected a six-year-old's activities and language. The characters of Dick and Jane represented Everyboy and Everygirl and first appeared in a 1930s Elson Basic Reader pre-primer. Because I was a visual learner, I was an active participant in my first-grade class's book discussions. As I read the pictures, I learned that Jane wore dresses and Dick did things! I learned that Mom was usually in the kitchen wearing an apron and holding the family together. The Dick and Jane books were retired when our concept of the family changed, but, interestingly, baby boomers who learned by that method grew up incorporating pictures into everything they did. For more information, read Carole and Marvin Heiferman's *Growing Up with Dick and Jane: Learning and Living the American Dream* (HarperCollins, 1996).

There are now many opportunities to view original book illustration. I saw a traveling exhibit of original art for the illustrations in the Dick and Jane series at the Norton Museum of Art in West Palm Beach, Florida, and then again at the Osborne Collection in Toronto, Canada. Special collections, such as the Eric Carle Museum of Picture Book Art, are dedicated to educating the public about book illustration. The following websites provide more information on illustrators and their art:

Society of Illustrators Museum of American Illustration, http://www. societyillustrators.org

National Center for Children's Illustrated Literature, http://www.nccil.org

Eric Carle Museum of Picture Book Art, http://www.picturebookart.org

Children's Literature, reviews and interviews with illustrators, http://www.childrenslit.com

Every Picture Tells a Story, online gallery of original illustrations, http://www.everypicture.com

International Board on Books for Young People, http://www.ibby.org

Picture Book, information about the book industry, http://www .picture-book.com

Bologna Children's Book Fair, http://www.publishers.asn.au/book_ fairs.cfm?doc_id=82

Also visit the individual web pages of children's book publishers.

In addition to exhibits, lectures by book illustrators offer insight into their work. They help us understand the collaborative process of making the book. We see a book in a new way when we hear about the process of creating it and learn about the materials and techniques used. What is more, visits and lectures by illustrators can build the self-esteem of children who crave encouragement in the arts.

Recently, in a program at the Portland Museum of Art, I heard David Macaulay tell about his process of working as an illustrator. He was able to show how drawings and ideas that do not quite work are as much a part of the creative process as those that do. Macaulay's presentation reminded me that children's librarians need to be doubly responsible to the public when selecting award books. If our choices do not meet the highest standards of excellence, our profession and the awards run the risk of becoming trivial. Macaulay also reminded the audience that although a book for children might be playful, there is very serious work behind it. To learn more from illustrators speaking on their own work, read Julie Cummins's *Wings of an Artist: Children's Book Illustrators Talk about Their Art* (Abrams, 1999) and Leonard Marcus's *Ways of Telling: Conversations on the Art of the Picture Book* (Dutton, 2002).

To enhance your visual literacy, do some of your own drawing or painting. Working with something as simple as a few crayons and a blank sheet of paper will break down your inhibitions. If we ask our children to do it, we can too. Use the workbook format of Marilyn J. S. Goodman and Natalie K. Lieberman's *Learning through Art: The Guggenheim Museum Collection* (Abrams, 2001) to break the ice and get you started. An exercise I suggest in my workshop is to look at Cassie in *Tar Beach,* by Faith Ringgold. Ringgold is concerned about expressing how Cassie feels, not about following rules of perspective. As you view the illustrations, make a self-portrait depicting how you feel. Forget about any "right" way to draw. Show yourself flying over your favorite places. Put in enough details to make your rendering of you and your special places distinctive. Ask a friend to read your picture. Based on your drawing, can your friend describe what you like and what makes you unique? Then ask yourself, "How can I improve my drawing to say what I mean?" Then you will begin to understand the challenge that illustrators face. For more inspiration, read Mila Boutan's *Monet: Art Activity Pack* (Chronicle Books, 1996). Art packs are also available for Cezanne, Degas, Gauguin, Matisse, Picasso, Renoir, and Van Gogh. Also take a look at *A Book of Artrageous Projects,* by Klutz Press and the Metropolitan Museum of Art (Klutz, 2000).

Modern painters such as Rothko, Motherwell, and Warhol deserve our attention because they have forged new territories and introduced us to new and sometimes uncomfortable feelings. Museums have retrospective shows to honor their work. Similarly, an illustrator award for a body of work acknowledges a lifetime of creative book illustration. Sometimes one of the books features a breakthrough design that can lead to even more exceptional work in the next book. An award for the body of an illustrator's work is the way to reward illustrations that are experimental. In contrast, when selecting a single book for an award for illustration, the collaborative nature of the book, the text, and the audience need to be considered. Therefore, the Caldecott Medal, in my opinion, is not exclusively for cutting-edge illustration.

When we take the time to really look at the pictures in books, know the elements of design, understand cultural context, and develop our visual literacy, we become well prepared to undertake our search for excellence. We can then celebrate picture book illustration with our hearts and our heads.

The Newbery Awards

2004—1922

2004 NEWBERY AWARD

THE TALE OF DESPEREAUX: BEING THE STORY OF A MOUSE, A PRINCESS, SOME SOUP, AND A SPOOL OF THREAD

Kate DiCamillo

Candlewick

KATE DICAMILLO

The Tale of Despereaux draws the reader into an enchanting account of a smaller-than-usual mouse in love with music, stories, and a princess named Pea. This tiny hero faints at loud noises but gathers the courage to fulfill his dreams.

With character and plot far more complex than the traditional fairy tale, separate stories introduce Despereaux, condemned for talking to the princess; the evil rat, Roscuro, who loves light and soup; and Miggery Sow, a farm girl with royal aspirations. Their fates are threaded together as Despereaux undertakes a hero's quest that culminates in mice, rats, and humans living almost happily ever after. The lyrical language of this distinctive tale is as savory as the palace soup.

"With finesse, DiCamillo masterfully weaves drama, mystery, and intrigue with high humor and fun into a cohesive, captivating, and distinguished tale," said Newbery Award Chair Eliza T. Dresang. "Time-honored themes of good versus evil, light versus dark, unrequited love, loyalty, and search for identity have roots in many mythic and literary classics familiar to children. This story is sure to entice, challenge, and delight readers of all ages."

2004 HONOR BOOKS

Olive's Ocean   Kevin Henkes   Greenwillow

Twelve-year-old Martha receives a page from the journal of a classmate, Olive, who has died in an accident. Olive's entry about a desire to be Martha's friend, to see the ocean, and to become a writer propels Martha into a journey from childhood to the brink of adolescence. Beautiful and powerful imagery drawn from the sun, sand, and sea of Martha's summer with her family and friends at Cape Cod skillfully reflects the pain and joy of Martha's coming-of-age and awareness of her own mortality.

Kevin Henkes's precision with language and elegant pacing allow him to juggle several layers of story with immediacy and subtlety that make the reader live the story. Henkes effectively captures the ebb and flow of early adolescence. This novel transforms a universal slice of life into an experience as enigmatic and compelling as the ocean itself.

An American Plague: The True and Terrifying Story of the Yellow Fever Epidemic of 1793   Jim Murphy   Clarion

An American Plague: The True and Terrifying Story of the Yellow Fever Epidemic of 1793 dramatically recounts the story of the yellow fever epidemic that nearly decimated the population of Philadelphia at the end of the eighteenth century. Details of the rapid, unstoppable spread of this dread disease make clear its far-reaching consequences for the political and social stability of the young republic and on the lives of the people involved. Integrating newspapers, diaries, personal testimonies, and period illustrations, the narrative delivers a social and medical history of the times and raises chilling questions about the disease today.

With superb verbal craftsmanship, Murphy conveys the tension of the mystery and impending doom of this epidemic, ending with the frightening fact of its contemporary relevance. The compelling narrative of investigation and unsolved mystery turns facts into a spell-binding story in an outstanding nonfiction presentation for a child audience.

2003 AWARD

Crispin: The Cross of Lead   Avi   Hyperion

Crispin: The Cross of Lead is an action-filled page-turner set in fourteenth-century England. "Asta's son" is the only name the thirteen-year-old title character has ever known when he is suddenly orphaned and stripped of home and possessions. Accused of murder and wanted dead or alive, Crispin flees his village and falls in with a juggler, Bear, who becomes his protector and teacher. Relentlessly pursued by Crispin's enemies, the pair flees to solve the mystery of his identity and fight the injustices of feudalism.

HONORS

The House of the Scorpion   Nancy Farmer   Atheneum

Farmer tackles the provocative topics of cloning, the value of life, illegal immigration, and the drug trade in a coming-of-age novel set in a desolate, futuristic desert.

Pictures of Hollis Woods   Patricia Reilly Giff   Random House

Twelve-year-old Hollis Woods unfolds her story of foster care and a search for family in images from her sketchbook, which reveal both her memories and her artistic soul. Strong visual imagery, multi-layered structure, and memorable characters create an emotionally satisfying story.

Hoot   Carl Hiaasen   Knopf

Hiaasen's wildly funny satire features the new kid, Roy, joining forces with tough Beatrice and the elusive Mullet Fingers to defeat a bully, thwart an avaricious corporation, and save a colony of burrowing owls. Hiaasen's work is both a rollicking adventure and a serious examination of values that threaten our environment.

A Corner of the Universe   Ann M. Martin   Scholastic

With the surprising arrival of a mentally disabled uncle, twelve-year-old Hattie Owen's world is turned upside down. Ann Martin used her own childhood memories to create a 1960s small-town setting, perfectly suited to this poignant story.

Surviving the Applewhites   Stephanie S. Tolan   HarperCollins

Tolan features pierced and spike-haired Jake, who has been expelled from every possible public school before his unwilling arrival at Wit's End, N.C., and the homeschool run by the chaotic and outrageous Applewhite family. The eccentric characters and fast pace culminate in a hilarious musical production that forces Jake to grow.

2002 AWARD

A Single Shard   Linda Sue Park   Houghton/Clarion

Park takes readers to twelfth-century Korea to tell a timeless story of dedication to one's dreams and art in A Single Shard. Tree-ear, an orphan, becomes fascinated with a nearby community of potters. Drawn by their exquisite craftsmanship, the adolescent boy begins to assist the master potter Min. Tree-ear's determination and bravery in pursuing his dream of becoming a potter take readers on a literary journey that demonstrates how courage, honor, and perseverance can overcome great odds and bring great happiness.

HONORS

Everything on a Waffle   Polly Horvath   Farrar Straus Giroux

When eleven-year-old Primrose Squarp's parents disappear at sea, her faith in their return defies all adult logic. Set in British Columbia, *Everything on a Waffle* combines quirky characters, recipes, and amazing twists of plot in a striking combination of the barely credible and profoundly true.

Carver: A Life in Poems   Marilyn Nelson   Front Street

Nelson challenges readers with a truly new biography of George Washington Carver. Told from multiple perspectives, this collection of fifty-nine poems reveals little-known facets of the remarkable scientist, who it too often dismissed as "the peanut man." With simple sophistication and beauty, Nelson transcends Carver's brilliance and scientific achievements to present the essence of this profoundly humble man.

2001 AWARD

A Year Down Yonder   Richard Peck   Dial Books for Young
Readers/Penguin Putnam

A linked series of vignettes set in rural Illinois during the Depression. *A Year Down Yonder* tells the story of fifteen-year-old Mary Alice who leaves Chicago to spend a year with Grandma Dowdel. Her initial apprehension about life in a small town with a scheming old woman gradually gives way to admiration and love as she recognizes the warm heart behind Grandma's shenanigans.

HONORS

Hope Was Here   Joan Bauer   Putnam

Hope Was Here relates how sixteen-year-old Hope and her aunt move to a small town in Wisconsin to join the "short order dance" of life at the Welcome

Stairways Diner. In the course of just a few months, Hope encounters issues as diverse as her customers: corruption in politics, a new love, serious illness, and the meaning of family.

The Wanderer   Sharon Creech   Joanna Cotler Books/a HarperCollins imprint

Sailing across the Atlantic with her uncles and cousins becomes a journey of discovery for thirteen-year-old Sophie. The carefully designed plot gradually reveals the truth of Sophie's past, even as readers begin to wonder about this rag-tag crew. Through journal entries, multiple viewpoints are woven into a story that speaks to the power of survival and the delicacy of grief.

Because of Winn-Dixie   Kate DiCamillo   Candlewick

When a stray dog appears almost magically in the midst of the produce section of the Winn-Dixie grocery store, he leads ten-year-old India Opal Buloni from one new friend to the next in a small Florida town. The stories she hears from each one help her to piece together a new definition of family.

Joey Pigza Loses Control   Jack Gantos   Farrar Straus Giroux

Spending the summer with his estranged father, Joey longs for the two of them to be winners together, but their lives gradually spiral out of control. As the old "wired" Joey returns, readers will long to see him regain his balance in an out-of-kilter world. Like many family stories, this is a tale whose pain is generously laced with humor.

2000 AWARD

Bud, Not Buddy   Christopher Paul Curtis   Delacorte

Ten-year-old Bud Caldwell runs away from a foster home and begins an unforgettable journey in search of his father. His only clues are old flyers left by his now-deceased mother that point to a legendary jazz bandleader. Bud's fast-paced first-person account moves with the rhythms of jazz and celebrates life, family, and a child's indomitable spirit.

HONORS

Getting Near to Baby   Audrey Couloumbis   Putnam

Twelve-year-old Willa Jo and Little Sister, whose voice is "lost in sadness," live with bossy Aunt Patty following the death of their baby sister. Willa Jo finds haven on the roof and from sunrise to sunset recalls recent events and helps her family come to terms with its tragedy.

Our Only May Amelia   Jennifer L. Holm   HarperCollins

Growing up as the only girl in a large Finnish-American farming family along Washington's Nasel River in 1899, 12-year-old May Amelia prefers tricks and adventures to being a "proper young lady." Unjustly blamed for tragedy, May must leave home before returning to claim her rightful place.

26 Fairmount Avenue   Tomie dePaola   Putnam

DePaola looks back to 1938 when his family, overcoming fire and flood, builds a new house. That year Tomie "quits" kindergarten, shares "chocolates" with Nana upstairs, critiques a movie, practices mural art, and finally moves to 26 Fairmount Avenue.

1999 AWARD

Holes   Louis Sachar   Frances Foster Books   Farrar Straus Giroux

Stanley Yelnats, the heir to his family's curse of bad luck, is convicted of a crime he didn't commit. He serves his sentence at Camp Green Lake, a dry, flat wasteland where the warden assigns each inmate the task of digging one hole every day. Hole by hole, Stanley and his friend Zero dig their destiny.

HONOR

A Long Way from Chicago   Richard Peck   Dial Books for Young Readers

An old man looks back on rollicking summers spent with his larger-than-life grandmother during the Great Depression in this colorful novel made up of seven masterfully interwoven tales.

1998 AWARD

Out of the Dust   Karen Hesse   Scholastic

Fourteen-year-old Billie Jo relates how her mother dies after an accident with burning kerosene. Blaming both herself and her father, she is unable to express herself through her piano playing because of the burns that scar her hands. She leaves but quickly returns to her home "of dust" and she realizes how much a part of her it is.

HONORS

Ella Enchanted   Gail Carson Levine   HarperCollins

Spunky, stubborn, and very clever, this new Cinderella spends a lifetime trying to outwit the curse of a fairy's unwelcome gift of obedience. In a kingdom populated with ogres, giants, princes, and fairies, Ella begins a fruitless quest to have the curse lifted, only to discover that she has that power within herself.

Lily's Crossing   Patricia Reilly Giff   Delacorte

During her 1944 summer vacation in the Rockaways, ten-year-old Lily's best friend moves away and her beloved father Poppy goes off to war. Then Lily meets Albert, a young Hungarian refugee with whom she builds a poignant friendship based on shared loneliness, secrets, and lies.

Wringer   Jerry Spinelli   HarperCollins

Palmer LaRue dreads his approaching birthday because he does not want to be a wringer, one of the ten-year-old boys who breaks the necks of pigeons wounded at the town's pigeon shoot fund-raiser. When his three bullying friends suspect he is sheltering a stray pigeon, Palmer decides to take a personal stand against this annual rite of passage.

1997 AWARD

The View from Saturday   E. L. Konigsburg   Jean Karl   Atheneum

Mrs. Olinski selects four of her sixth-grade students to be the Academic Bowl team. No one understands her choice of these particular students, including Mrs. Olinski, who continues to question herself. The students surprise everyone with their unique contributions to the challenges of competition.

HONORS

A Girl Named Disaster   Nancy Farmer   Jackson/Orchard

When Nhamo (Disaster) flees her village to search for her father in Zimbabwe, she is lost on Lake Cabora Bassa in Mozambique. Alone, she survives harsh weather, wild animals, and near starvation before building a new life in the world of her father's people.

Moorchild   Eloise McGraw   Margaret K. McElderry   Simon & Schuster

Moorchild Moql becomes the changeling Saaski, half-human, half-Folk, and an outcast in both worlds. The reader is drawn into the lives of the moorfolk who fear Saaski and those who try to understand her and support her.

The Thief   Megan Whalen Turner   Greenwillow

Freed from the royal dungeons and commanded to steal an ancient talisman from supernatural guardians, young Gen pulls off an astonishing scam and in the process rescues his own country from a threatened invasion.

Belle Prater's Boy   Ruth White   Farrar Straus Giroux

Gypsy's cousin Woodrow comes to live next door, bringing with him a mystery and the key to a secret that Gypsy keeps from herself. Grandparents and Gypsy's supportive mother and stepfather create a loving environment in which the children can come to grips with their losses.

1996 AWARD

The Midwife's Apprentice   Karen Cushman   Clarion

The central character, Brat, is a homeless waif who first appears sleeping in a dung heap "unwashed, unnourished, unloved, and unlovely . . . ." From a person with no hopes, no dreams, and no expectations she becomes the midwife's apprentice—a person with a name and a place in the world. An excellent portrayal of medieval England.

HONORS

What Jamie Saw   Carolyn Coman   Front Street

What Jamie Saw is a gripping interior novel that portrays a desperate mother and her quietly heroic son as they move from an impossibly bleak situation toward a promise of hope. Coman captures Jamie's fear, his uncertainty, and his confusion as well as his growing confidence and ability to stand up for himself.

The Watsons Go to Birmingham—1963   Christopher Paul Curtis   Delacorte

From its hilarious opening chapters to its shattering conclusion, *The Watsons Go to Birmingham* is a compelling novel that brings to life an African-American family. It draws together everyday events in such a way as to send the Watsons on a journey to Birmingham that will change them forever. The depiction of devastating events in Birmingham integrates the dichotomy of familial love and stability with the racial strife of the 1960s.

Yolonda's Genius   Carol Fenner   Margaret K. McElderry   Simon & Schuster

Fenner portrays memorable characters and a vivid, authentic place in this engaging story of a bright, feisty fifth grader. Yolonda is determined to bring to light her younger brother's extraordinary talent of transforming the world around him into the music he makes.

The Great Fire   Jim Murphy   Scholastic

The riveting narrative of the 1871 Chicago fire thrusts the reader into the center of the raging conflagration. Murphy weaves eyewitness accounts of the disaster with factual and social commentary, period photographs, etchings, and maps into memorable nonfiction writing.

1995 AWARD

Walk Two Moons   Sharon Creech   HarperCollins

Thirteen-year-old Salamanca Tree Hiddle sets out on a cross-country journey with her grandparents to see her mother, who has not returned from a visit to Idaho. Sal entertains her grandparents by telling them about her new friend Phoebe, and in so doing begins to understand herself and her own mother. The book, packed with humor and affection, is an odyssey of unexpected twists and surprising conclusions.

HONORS

Catherine, Called Birdy   Karen Cushman   Clarion

> In the course of her fourteenth year, Catherine keeps a journal of her perceptive observations and longings for adventure and independence. Her lively, humorous descriptions of life on a thirteenth century English manor, midst unwanted suitors and ever-present fleas, reach through to time to speak to modern readers.

The Ear, the Eye, and the Arm   Nancy Farmer   Jackson/Orchard

> A kidnapping of the General's three children in twenty-second-century Zimbabwe sets off a dramatic chase. In a series of extraordinary adventures, the children play a crucial role in a thrilling battle against the forces of evil. This futuristic detective story is interwoven with African's history, present-day concerns, and a variety of colorful characters.

1994 AWARD

The Giver   Lois Lowry   Houghton

Twelve-year-old Jonas performs well in the impressively ordered society that the Elders have developed. But when he is selected to be the new "Receiver," Jonas begins to unravel the truth that underlies his world.

HONORS

Crazy Lady   Jane Leslie Conly   HarperCollins

> Twelve-year-old Vernon's initially reluctant, off-beat friendship with an alcoholic and her developmentally disabled son has repercussions throughout the neighborhood, changing the lives of all involved. The reader becomes aware that Vernon's growing self-esteem and maturity come about through his commitment to helping his friends.

Eleanor Roosevelt: A Life of Discovery Russell Freedman Clarion

Through compelling text and contemporary photographs, Eleanor Roosevelt is shown moving from a sheltered, unhappy childhood to the world's stage. This fascinating biography of a remarkable and complex woman is meticulously researched.

Dragon's Gate Laurence Yep HarperCollins

Dragon's Gate is a carefully researched, well-written account of the lives of the Chinese who built the transcontinental railroad in the Sierra Mountains. This glimpse into the complex working community of California at the time of the Civil War is also a sensitive portrayal of the relationship between a father and son.

1993 AWARD

Missing May Cynthia Rylant Jackson/Orchard

Twelve-year-old Summer lives with her Aunt May and Uncle Ob in the mountains of West Virginia. When May dies, Summer, Uncle Ob, and Summer's friend, Cletus, try to get her back—or at least to get word of her—and to alleviate the pain. This trio of lovingly described characters journeys from intense grief to the understanding that love is never truly lost.

HONORS

What Hearts Bruce Brooks A Laura Geringer Book, a HarperCollins imprint

Seven-year-old Asa, by far the best in his class, comes home from the last day of school with a knapsack full of prizes to find that his whole world has changed. Asa tries to make sense of a world in which he is challenged and put down by a domineering stepfather and only partially sustained by his loving but disturbed mother. Four stories show Asa at seven, nine, eleven, and twelve, struggling to find the secret of connection with others.

The Dark-thirty: Southern Tales of the Supernatural
Patricia C. McKissack Knopf

The dark-thirty is that special half hour of twilight, just before dark, when everyone hurries home because the spirits and monsters come out. This collection of spine-tingling tales ranges from the time of slavery to the civil rights movement. Strong characterization, classic themes, and suspenseful plots are strongly crafted in the oral tradition of African-American folklore.

Somewhere in the Darkness Walter Dean Myers Scholastic

Jimmy Little had always wanted a father. However, when Crab, his father, who is virtually a stranger, appears in a dark hallway straight from a prison hospital, it is not at all what he had hoped for. On the tense, frightening trip with Crab to Chicago and then to Alabama, Jimmy finds he must learn self-knowledge as well as compassion to deal with a difficult and dangerous situation.

1992 AWARD

Shiloh   Phyllis Reynolds Naylor/Atheneum

Marty Preston, an eleven-year-old West Virginian boy, befriends a stray dog and while protecting the dog from abuse wrestles with universal questions of honesty, commitment, and ethical decision making. Marty discovers that discerning right from wrong is not as straightforward as he had imagined.

HONORS

Nothing But the Truth: A Documentary Novel   Avi   Jackson/Orchard

Avi's documentary approach chronicles the results of a teacher's objection to a ninth grader's humming along with "The Star Spangled Banner." School rules stipulate that students are to stand at "respectful, silent attention." Miscommunication, misperceptions, and personal viewpoints of right, wrong, and protected freedoms propel the characters rapidly into a crisis situation that forces the reader to explore issues of perception, reality, bias, and expediency.

The Wright Brothers: How They Invented the Airplane
Russell Freedman   Holiday House

In a spirited blend of science, history, and biography, Freedman presents a fascinating portrait of a new age. Using Wilber and Orville Wright's own photographs as well as excerpts from their notes and journals, he creates a uniquely personal and engaging view of their accomplishments.

1991 AWARD

Maniac Magee   Jerry Spinelli   Little, Brown

Jeffrey Lionel Magee is a legendary character who runs the rails faster than other kids run the ground. Jeffrey bunts "the world's first frogball for a four-bagger" and performs other amazing feats.

HONOR

The True Confessions of Charlotte Doyle   Avi   Jackson/Orchard

Avi weaves a finely crafted tale of high seas adventure and gripping suspense, made rich by thirteen-year-old Charlotte's deepening understanding of honor and herself.

1990 AWARD

Number the Stars Lois Lowry Houghton

When ten-year-old Annemarie Johansen's family decides to pretend that her friend Ellen Rosen is her sister, they become involved in the effort to save the Danish Jews from the Nazis. As the author deftly portrays deep friendship, a strong family, and heroism in wartime, the story builds to a tense climax.

HONORS

Afternoon of the Elves Janet Taylor Lisle Jackson/Orchard

Fascinated by Sarah-Kate's backyard elf village, Hillary is unprepared for the secret side of the older girl's life. Strong, tough, an outcast at school, Sarah-Kate has been doing whatever she must to care for herself and her mentally ill mother. When her plight is discovered by adults, disturbing but necessary changes occur.

The Winter Room Gary Paulsen Jackson/Orchard

From the first page to the last, this story of farm life in northern Minnesota is so engrossing that the place and the people seem real. Eldon, the eleven-year-old narrator, takes the reader through the seasons and into the winter room, where stories are "not for believing so much, as to be believed in."

Shabanu, Daughter of the Wind Suzanne Fisher Staples Knopf

Spirited and courageous Shabanu, younger daughter of present-day Pakistani camel herders, loves her family's life and her role in caring for their camels. Both Shabanu and her older sister are betrothed to brothers, but as her sister's wedding nears, a calamity occurs that changes forever the life of independent Shabanu.

1989 AWARD

Joyful Noise: Poems for Two Voices Paul Fleischman
Illustrated by Eric Beddows Zolotow/Harper

Fourteen poems, using two voices, sometimes alternating, sometimes together, offer listeners a look at what insects just might think of themselves and their world. The book lice, grasshoppers, house crickets, and their poetic companions are illustrated in soft yet often comical black-and-white pencil drawings.

HONORS

In the Beginning: Creation Stories from Around the World
Virginia Hamilton Illustrated by Barry Moser Harcourt

Stories from African, Chinese, Native American, and Guinean peoples are represented among the twenty-five creation myths found in this collection. Faithfully retold, the stories are followed by notes about their sources. Dramatic watercolor paintings accent each tale.

Scorpions   Walter Dean Myers   Harper

Hoping to find a way to raise money for an appeal for his imprisoned older brother, twelve-year-old Jamal agrees to try to become the leader of his brother's Harlem gang, the Scorpions. Involvement with the gang (and the gun he is given) leads to tragedy for Jamal and his friend Tito.

1988 AWARD

Lincoln: A Photobiography   Russell Freedman   Clarion

An ambitious man, Lincoln struggled hard to get an education, to build his law practice, and to become politically successful. The man, his wit, and his wisdom are vividly and honestly portrayed in this straightforward biography and its ninety photographs.

HONORS

After the Rain   Norma Fox Mazer   Morrow

Fifteen-year-old Rachel tries to balance her concern for her own life with her grandfather's need for her help. Never close to the old man, she slowly comes to love him. As she struggles to help him maintain his independence, he weakens and nears death.

Hatchet   Gary Paulsen   Bradbury

When the pilot dies of a heart attack, Brian crash-lands the small plane in the Canadian wilderness. Left with only a hatchet and the clothes he is wearing, Brian begins a gripping fifty-four-day ordeal that challenges his physical and psychological skills to their limits.

1987 AWARD

The Whipping Boy   Sid Fleischman
Illustrated by Peter Sís   Greenwillow

Whenever Prince Brat does anything bad, Jemmy, his whipping boy, is punished. The spoiled prince decides to run away from the palace, forcing Jemmy to go with him. Far from the safety of the court, the prince quickly learns how little he knows about the outside world and how important Jemmy is to his survival.

HONORS

On My Honor   Marion Dane Bauer   Clarion

Before leaving on a bike ride with his impetuous friend Tony, Joel gives his father his word of honor that he will not swim in a river known to be dangerous. Tony convinces Joel that the river is safe; the two swim; and Tony drowns. Joel is left alone to face his guilt, both sets of parents, and his own grief.

Volcano: The Eruption and Healing of Mount St. Helens
Patricia Lauber   Bradbury

The eruption of Mount St. Helens and the subsequent regrowth of plants are vividly portrayed in color photographs and a dynamic text. The volcanic eruption is seen not as just a disaster, but as a builder of life on this planet.

A Fine White Dust   Cynthia Rylant   Bradbury

Although neither his parents nor his best friend are particularly religious, Peter feels a need for something deeper than just churchgoing. When an itinerant preacher comes to town, Peter is mesmerized by the man and "saved." Invited to go away with the preacher, Peter reluctantly agrees, only to be left behind and forgotten.

1986 AWARD

Sarah Plain and Tall   Patricia MacLachlan   Zolotow/Harper

Life on the prairie with two children and no wife is lonely and difficult, so Caleb and Anna's father advertises for a wife. Sarah answers his ad and soon agrees to come all the way from Maine for a visit. Captivated by her, Anna and Caleb worry that Sarah misses the sea too much to stay with them.

HONORS

Commodore Perry in the Land of the Shogun   Rhoda Blumberg   Lothrop

Commodore Perry's fascinating mission to Japan in 1853 is told at a lively pace, with special attention given to the negotiating skill that led to his success; to his sensitivity to cultural differences; and to his just plain curiosity. The accompanying pictures include many sketched by the Japanese and the Americans who were with Matthew Perry.

Dogsong   Gary Paulsen   Bradbury

Unhappy with the snowmobile-and-television society that seems to have taken over his Eskimo village, Russell turns to Oogruk, the old man of the village, for help in finding a path back to the old ways. With Oogruk's advice and encouragement, Russell begins an arduous dogsled journey northward to find his own "song."

1985 AWARD

The Hero and the Crown   Robin McKinley   Greenwillow

The daughter of the king of Damar and his second wife (a witch woman from the north), Aerin does not fit in at court. Unable to succeed her father to the throne, she must instead find her own destiny. Wielding her blue sword, she not only defeats dragons but finally becomes the hero of the kingdom.

HONORS

The Moves Make the Man   Bruce Brooks   Harper

The first black to go to the formerly all-white junior high school, Jerome is a passionate basketball player. When he meets Bix Rivers, an unstable outsider who is a gifted athlete, Jerome decides to teach him basketball. As they play the game, Bix's mental illness becomes more apparent, and Jerome is less able to help him.

One-Eyed Cat   Paula Fox   Bradbury

After his minister father takes his new air rifle away from him and puts it in the attic, Ned sneaks upstairs, takes it, fires it once, and is terrified that he may have hit a cat. Struggling with his guilt, he tells one lie after another until he cannot bear it anymore and must confess to someone.

Like Jake and Me   Mavis Jukes   Illustrated by Lloyd Bloom   Knopf

Alex wants to be liked by his rugged cowboy stepfather, but there are still barriers between the two. When Alex notices a wolf spider on Jake's neck and calmly mentions it, the rugged cowboy totally panics, admitting his terror of spiders. Alex comes to the rescue, and the two finally come to appreciate each other and their differences.

1984 AWARD

Dear Mr. Henshaw   Beverly Cleary
Illustrated by Paul O. Zelinsky   Morrow

Leigh Botts starts writing to the author of *Ways to Amuse a Dog* in second grade. Year after year the letters, and then a diary, become vehicles for expressing his feelings about himself, his parents' divorce, and his problems in school. Leigh's growth and acceptance of the divorce are tempered with much humor.

HONORS

The Wish Giver: Three Tales of Coven Tree   Bill Brittain
Illustrated by Andrew Glass   Harper

> Thaddeus Blinn, the wish giver, sells Polly, Rowena, Henry, and Stew Meat wishes. All they have to do is hold the white card with the dot and wish carefully. The first three make their wishes with dire but comical consequences and leave Stew Meat to use his to undo everything they have done.

Sugaring Time   Kathryn Lasky
Photographs by Christopher G. Knight   Macmillan

> The author and photographer record a family's old-fashioned method of sugaring. When the right time finally comes, family members tap the maple trees, boil the sap, and enjoy a sugar-on-snow party and a pancake breakfast. The family's enjoyment of sugaring is evident in the often poetic text and the clear black-and-white photographs.

The Sign of the Beaver   Elizabeth George Speare   Houghton

> Left alone in the Maine wilderness, Matt first loses his rifle and food and then is savagely stung by bees. Found by Saknis, chief of the Beaver tribe, Matt is cared for in exchange for teaching the chief's grandson to read. As the boys' friendship develops, Matt gains an appreciation for the heritage and skills of the Beaver tribe.

A Solitary Blue   Cynthia Voigt   Atheneum

> Abandoned at the age of seven by his cause-conscious mother, Jeff is left to fend for himself and take care of his absent-minded-professor father. Not until Jeff is stricken with pneumonia at the age of twelve does his father understand how he, too, has deserted his son. Slowly the two build a close, strong relationship that is able to help them survive and grow.

1983 AWARD

Dicey's Song   Cynthia Voigt   Atheneum

Finally settled in with Gram Tillerman while their mother is in a mental hospital, Dicey and her brothers and sisters discover that it is not easy to become a family. They must learn to love and trust Gram—and she them—while they try to adjust to a new school and make friends.

HONORS

Graven Images   Paul Fleischman   Illustrated by Andrew Glass   Harper

Three gripping stories, two sinister and one funny and all with historical settings, are centered on graven images: a wooden boy with a frightening secret, a weathervane that leads to true love, and a statue ordered by a ghost.

Homesick: My Own Story   Jean Fritz   Illustrated by Margot Tomes   Putnam

Fritz remembers with humor and poignancy two years of her childhood in China during the turbulent 1920s. She contends with being a "foreign devil," losing a longed-for baby sister, and, most of all, longing for the United States, a country she has never seen.

Sweet Whispers, Brother Rush   Virginia Hamilton   Philomel

Life changes radically for fourteen-year-old Tree and her older retarded brother when the ghost of Brother Rush appears to Tree, first in the street and then in her home. The handsome ghost of her mother's brother takes her back in time to bear witness to the past and to learn about the terrible disease that is killing her own brother.

The Blue Sword   Robin McKinley   Greenwillow

Angharad Crewe is yanked out of an easy life on a Homelander outpost and thrust into one of rigorous training for her prophesied role as deliverer of the Hillfolk. She earns the right to carry the Blue Sword into battle, and with it she heroically leads a small band of warriors against the nonhuman Northerners.

Doctor De Soto   William Steig   Farrar

As mice dentists, the diminutive De Sotos have always refused to treat dangerous animals until a miserable fox appears begging for help. The compassionate mice cleverly find a way to rid the fox of his pain while guaranteeing their own safety.

1982 AWARD

A Visit to William Blake's Inn: Poems for Innocent and Experienced Travelers   Nancy Willard
Illustrated by Alice and Martin Provensen   Harcourt

Written in the spirit of William Blake, these magical poems are built around the visit of a child to Blake's inn. It is staffed by mighty dragons that brew and bake, angels that wash feather beds, and animals that dance to the music of the Marmalade Man.

HONORS

Ramona Quimby, Age 8   Beverly Cleary
Illustrated by Alan Tiegreen   Morrow

> Ramona is now starting the third grade and her life is full of the usual hilarious trials that cause her to be labeled a "nuisance and show-off" by her new teacher. Whether she is deciding she prefers her printed Q to the floppy cursive one, getting raw egg in her hair, or facing an interminably boring Sunday, Ramona is always a memorable character.

Upon the Head of the Goat: A Childhood in Hungary 1939–1944
Aranka Siegal   Farrar

> The destruction of nine-year-old Piri's family begins with Hungary's occupation by the Nazis. Her mother valiantly tries to keep the family together and safe, but one loss after another occurs until they board trains that will take them to Auschwitz. Siegal's book is a powerful autobiography.

1981 AWARD

Jacob Have I Loved   Katherine Paterson   Crowell

Although she takes pride in her twin sister's singing talent, Wheeze (Louise) is jealous of the attention Caroline gets on their Chesapeake Bay island. It is only when she leaves and starts a life as a midwife in Kentucky that Wheeze comes to understand that she has always been loved and accepted for herself.

HONORS

The Fledgling   Jane Langton   Illustrated by Erik Blegvad   Harper

> Frail young Georgie, almost light enough to blow away, is obsessed with her belief that she can fly. When a large Canada goose she has befriended hoots outside her window, Georgie hops on his back and flies away. Night after night they soar above Walden Pond until one misfortune and then another end Georgie's flying forever.

A Ring of Endless Light   Madeleine L'Engle   Farrar

> Sixteen-year-old Vicky and her family spend the summer on a New England island with her dying grandfather. All summer long she and her family are preoccupied with the mysteries of life, death, and eternity, yet there is still time for Vicky to help with a Marine Biology Station dolphin project and to date two boys.

1980 AWARD

A Gathering of Days: A New England Girl's Journal, 1830–1832
Joan W. Blos   Scribner

Catherine Cabot Hall sporadically writes in her journal, filling it with recipes, excerpts from her copy book, secrets, fears, confidences, details of her adjustment to her stepmother, and thoughts on the pain of a friend's death. Though fiction, the journal is believable, and Catherine is easy to like.

HONOR

The Road from Home: The Story of an Armenian Girl
David Kherdian   Greenwillow

> After the Turks finish with their slaughter of nearly two million Armenians, Veron is the only survivor of her immediate family. When the Greeks attack Turkey, Veron and her aunt and cousin escape to Greece, and from there she travels to the United States, a mail-order bride and the future mother of the author.

1979 AWARD

The Westing Game   Ellen Raskin   Dutton

An expensive apartment building mysteriously fills up with sixteen occupants—all named as heirs or possible murderers in millionaire Sam Westing's will. The sixteen are paired, given $10,000, and challenged to discover who really killed Sam Westing.

HONOR

The Great Gilly Hopkins   Katherine Paterson   Crowell

> Abandoned as a preschooler, Gilly has gone through a succession of foster homes. Smart, self-sufficient, and superficially hard, Gilly manages to do just what she wants until she is sent to stay with Maime Trotter, a woman with a big heart, patience, and wisdom enough to know how to reach the unhappy girl.

1978 AWARD

Bridge to Terabithia   Katherine Paterson
Illustrated by Donna Diamond   Crowell

After practicing all summer to be the fastest runner in school, Jess is beaten by the new girl, Leslie. Gradually the two become close friends, creating an imaginary world in the woods and calling it Terabithia. When tragedy strikes, Jess, shocked and despairing, slowly begins to see the wonders Leslie left him.

HONORS

Ramona and Her Father   Beverly Cleary
Illustrated by Alan Tiegreen   Morrow

> Ramona is in second grade when her father loses his job and her mother begins to work full-time. Ramona tries her best to help her family through the crisis, even starting a campaign to get her father to quit smoking. Her worries, problems, and joys, presented with lively good humor, are common to many children her age.

Anpao: An American Indian Odyssey   Jamake Highwater
Illustrated by Fritz Scholder   Lippincott

> A beautiful Indian maiden promises to marry Anpao, but first he must get the Sun's permission and have him remove the ugly scar on his face. As Anpao travels the world looking for the Sun, he hears stories about his own roots as well as legends and myths of his people.

1977 AWARD

Roll of Thunder, Hear My Cry   Mildred D. Taylor   Dial

Cassie Logan and her brothers are part of a warm, intelligent, and courageous black family in rural Mississippi during the Depression. They try to maintain their pride as they take abuse from white children and then recognize that their personal difficulties are only symptoms of greater problems within their community.

HONORS

A String in the Harp   Nancy Bond   Atheneum

> Their father's remoteness and the strangeness of school in Wales make the children's adjustment to their mother's death even more difficult. Then twelve-year-old Peter finds an ancient harp key that pulls him back into Welsh history, helping him discover a purpose to living.

Abel's Island   William Steig   Farrar

> After a violent storm, Abel, a mouse, finds himself alone, bewildered, and far, far away from his beloved wife Amanda. Sustained by his love for his wife, Abel uses all his resources to survive for a year on the deserted island.

1976 AWARD

The Grey King   Susan Cooper
Illustrated by Michael Heslop   McElderry/Atheneum

In Wales recovering from a serious illness, eleven-year-old Will, the youngest of the Old Ones, uses his considerable powers to find the golden harp that will awaken the Sleepers. It is not an easy quest, and Will has only the mysterious Bran and Bran's dog, Cafall, to help him fight the forces of dark and evil.

HONORS

The Hundred Penny Box   Sharon Bell Mathis
Illustrated by Leo and Diane Dillon   Viking

> For each of her hundred years there is a penny in Aunt Dew's box and a story to go along with it. More than his parents, Michael understands the importance of the box to the old woman and loves to hear her tell the stories again and again.

Dragonwings   Laurence Yep   Harper

> In 1903 Moonshadow leaves the Middle Kingdom to join his father in San Francisco. To make the father's dream of building an aeroplane come true, the two of them leave the close-knit community that shelters their Chinese culture to live among white demons. Humorous accommodations are made between the different cultures as they grow in understanding and friendship.

1975 AWARD

M. C. Higgins, the Great   Virginia Hamilton   Macmillan

Up on Sarah's Mountain, M. C. dreams of a way for his family to escape the spoil heap that may one day destroy their home. It is not his dreams but the boy's own strength and determination that help the family find a way to keep themselves safe.

HONORS

My Brother Sam Is Dead   James Lincoln Collier and
Christopher Collier   Four Winds

> Tim's older brother, Sam, defies their father and runs off to join the Continental Army. When their father is imprisoned by the rebels and dies and Sam is hung by his own army, Tim sees how devastating war can be.

Philip Hall Likes Me, I Reckon Maybe   Bette Greene
Illustrated by Charles Lilly   Dial

> Eleven-year-old Beth Lambert, a spunky heroine, realizes she has been letting Philip Hall be number one in school because she is afraid he will not like her if she surpasses him. With gentle prodding from her family, Beth decides to go ahead and do her best—even if it means beating Philip Hall.

The Perilous Gard   Elizabeth Marie Pope
Illustrated by Richard Cuffari   Houghton

> Banished by Queen Mary to the remote castle of Elvenwood, Kate Sutton quickly learns the castle's secret: It guards the last practitioners of the old religions. To keep their power, the fairy folk decide to sacrifice the man Kate loves on All Hallow's Eve.

Figgs & Phantoms   Ellen Raskin   Dutton

> Mona is embarrassed by her zany, ex-show business family—except for her four-foot-four-inch-tall Uncle Florence Italy Figg. When he dies, Mona is desolate. She is sure he has gone to Capri, the Figg family Heaven, and decides to follow him.

1974 AWARD

The Slave Dancer   Paula Fox   Illustrated by Eros Keith   Bradbury

Kidnapped and forced to play his fife while the slaves "dance," thirteen-year-old Jessie learns all too soon about the savagery of the slave trade. For four long months he lives with the crew's cruelty until a storm wrecks the ship and Jessie and Ras, a would-be slave, are the only survivors.

HONOR

The Dark Is Rising   Susan Cooper
Illustrated by Alan Cober   McElderry/Atheneum

> On midwinter's eve, Will's eleventh birthday, the world is in turmoil with strange creatures appearing and stranger things happening. Will, the last of the Old Ones to be born, must use all his knowledge and skill to help in the fight against the Dark.

1973 AWARD

Julie of the Wolves Jean Craighead George
Illustrated by John Schoenherr Harper

Having run away from a forced marriage, thirteen-year-old Miyax, an Eskimo, becomes lost on the Arctic plain. Her only hope for survival is acceptance by a wolf pack. Imitating their facial expressions and body movements, Miyax slowly becomes one of them, while still trying to get to safety.

HONORS

Frog and Toad Together Arnold Lobel Harper

Whether they are testing their willpower with a bowl of cookies or their patience while waiting for seeds to grow, Frog and Toad delight in each other's company. Witty, easy-to-read, and full of warmth and gentle humor, these five stories engagingly explore the meaning of friendship.

The Upstairs Room Johanna Reiss Crowell

As the German occupation of Holland tightens, two Jewish sisters are forced to hide in a secret upstairs room in an old farmhouse for two years. The girls experience fear, hope, terror, and boredom in their daily life and depend on the kindness and courage of others for their survival.

The Witches of Worm Zilpha Keatley Snyder
Illustrated by Alton Raible Atheneum

Deserted by her friends and her mother, Jessica channels her anger at life into "evil acts" that her cat, Worm, supposedly forces her to perform. Convinced first that Worm is a witch's cat, then that she is a witch, Jessica is ultimately forced to face herself and her feelings.

1972 AWARD

Mrs. Frisby and the Rats of NIMH Robert C. O'Brien
Illustrated by Zena Bernstein Atheneum

When nothing she does seems to help her son Timothy get well, Mrs. Frisby, a widowed mouse, turns to a colony of super-intelligent rats for help. The rats' high intelligence is the result of experiments performed upon them by human scientists at NIMH. Now the rats are intent upon starting a new civilization free from human interference.

HONORS

Incident at Hawk's Hill   Allan W. Eckert
Illustrated by John Schoenherr   Little, Brown

Lonely, small, and frail, six-year-old Ben shies away from people but shows deep interest in and affinity toward animals. Lost during a storm, he takes refuge with a badger who has just lost her young. The badger adopts him, and he lives a feral life for three months until he is found. Convincingly written, the incident is based on an actual occurrence in 1870.

The Planet of Junior Brown   Virginia Hamilton   Macmillan

For more than two months, huge, musical genius Junior Brown and his friend and protector Buddy Clark have been cutting classes and hiding in a secret basement room created by the school custodian. Buddy and Mr. Poole, the custodian, are trying desperately to help Junior, who seems to be slipping slowly but inexorably into madness.

The Tombs of Atuan   Ursula K. LeGuin
Illustrated by Gail Garraty   Atheneum

From the time Tenar was five, her life has been focused on the tombs and her future as their priestess. Renamed Arha, she guards the labyrinthine tunnels, knowing that they hide great treasure. When she finds a man (Ged of *A Wizard of Earthsea*) in the tunnels seeking the other half to the Ring of Erreth-Akbe, Arha is torn between her duty to kill him and her compassion for him.

Annie and the Old One   Miska Miles
Illustrated by Peter Parnall   Little, Brown

Annie likes her life the way it is with her mother weaving, her father making jewelry, and her grandmother, the Old One, always there to tell her stories and to help with chores. When grandmother announces that she will die when the new rug is finished, Annie tries desperately to stop the inevitable by secretly unraveling the rug.

The Headless Cupid   Zilpha Keatley Snyder
Illustrated by Alton Raible   Atheneum

Eleven-year-old David is pleased about his father's remarriage until he meets his new stepsister, Amanda, a self-proclaimed witch. Angry at her mother for remarrying, Amanda sets up situations that lead the other children to believe their house is haunted. Then unexplained events turn the tables, frightening even Amanda.

1971 AWARD

Summer of the Swans   Betsy Byars   Illustrated by Ted CoConis   Viking

An insecure fourteen-year-old, Sarah is unhappy with herself and her family. Though she loves her mentally disabled brother Charlie, Sarah is tired of always being responsible for him. When Charlie turns up missing, however, Sarah tries desperately to find him and in the process discovers that she is less the ugly duckling than she had supposed.

HONORS

Knee Knock Rise   Natalie Babbitt   Farrar

In this tale filled with folk humor, Egan goes to the village for a visit and becomes intrigued with the tales and wails of a monster that lives in the peaks of Knee Knock Rise. After an unprecedented climb up the mountain, Egan discovers the practical explanation for the legendary creature. The villagers refuse to listen to him, preferring to let their folklore live on as history.

Enchantress from the Stars   Sylvia Louise Engdahl
Illustrated by Rodney Shackell   Atheneum

Invaded by technologically advanced Imperials, the Andrecians are close to being destroyed by their occupiers when beings from an even more highly advanced civilization decide to intervene secretly. Using their telekenetic powers, three Federation members pose as magicians, teaching a young Andrecian how to use his psychic abilities to combat the invaders.

Sing Down the Moon   Scott O'Dell   Houghton

At fourteen, Bright Morning dares to be optimistic about her future. Her mother is a wealthy Navajo, and Bright Morning is to marry Tall Boy, a young Navajo warrior. Then she is wrenched from her home by Spanish slavers. When freed, she is uprooted again, this time by the cavalry, who force the Navajo to make a 300-mile march to Bosque Redondo.

1970 AWARD

Sounder   William H. Armstrong   Illustrated by James Barkley   Harper

Sounder, the family dog, valiantly defends the father when the sheriff and his deputies come to arrest him for stealing food for his starving family. Years later, the dog, shot and maimed by the deputies, is the only one to recognize the father when he returns, paralyzed and deformed.

HONORS

Our Eddie   Sulamith Ish-Kishor   Pantheon

> Eddie's father is a stern, insensitive zealot who refuses, until it is too late, to see that his son is gradually succumbing to a debilitating disease. Set in London and New York in the 1920s, most of this story of a warm Jewish immigrant family is told by Eddie's insightful sister.

The Many Ways of Seeing: An Introduction to the Pleasures of Art
Janet Gaylord Moore   Illustrated with black-and-white and
color reproductions and photographs   World

> Moore, of the Cleveland Museum of Art, encourages readers to try a new way of approaching art: to see art reflecting the world and nature, and the world in turn reflecting art. Paintings (reproduced in color), poems, and quotations are arranged to lead to the discovery of new comparisons between modern, traditional, or ancient art and the imagery of word and picture.

Journey Outside   Mary Q. Steele   Illustrated by Rocco Negri   Viking

> In a story filled with allegory and symbolism, Dilar's people endlessly travel an underground river, headed for the "better place." But Dilar, suspecting that they are merely going around in circles, jumps from his raft and accidentally makes his way into the outside world. There, nearly blinded by the light, he tries to learn more about his people and to find a way to bring them aboveground.

1969 AWARD

The High King   Lloyd Alexander   Holt

In the final book of the chronicles of Prydain, Taran leads his forces against Arawn and his army of the dead. Victorious, but with great loss of life and destruction to Prydain, Taran becomes High King, fulfilling the predictions of his wizard guardian, Dallben.

HONORS

To Be a Slave   Julius Lester   Illustrated by Tom Feelings   Dial

> American slaves, runaways, and emancipated people provide a powerful testament of how they felt about slavery and what they endured. The author dynamically blends quotations from published and unpublished sources and presents them in rough chronological order.

When Shlemiel Went to Warsaw and Other Stories   Isaac Bashevis Singer
Illustrated by Margot Zemach   Farrar

> In eight delightfully silly stories, five retold from the Yiddish and three original, readers are introduced to a memorable collection of characters. Among them are a mixed-up Shlemiel, who does not recognize his wife and village, and Utzel's daughter, Poverty, who seems to grow larger as he grows poorer.

1968 AWARD

From the Mixed-Up Files of Mrs. Basil E. Frankweiler
E. L. Konigsburg   Atheneum

Having carefully planned how and to where they will run away, Claudia and her little brother, James (and his money), board a bus, head to New York City, and go to the Metropolitan Museum of Art. There they hide in washrooms, sleep on ancient beds, and get involved in solving an exciting mystery.

HONORS

Jennifer, Hecate, Macbeth, William McKinley, and Me, Elizabeth
E. L. Konigsburg   Atheneum

> Elizabeth is lonely at her new school until she meets Jennifer, a girl her age who claims to be a real witch. In awe of Jennifer, Elizabeth agrees to become her apprentice and initially finds her boring life full of adventure. But Jennifer is very demanding, and even superficially docile Elizabeth can only be pushed so far.

The Black Pearl   Scott O'Dell
Illustrated by Milton Johnson   Houghton

> In this story written with stark simplicity and riveting suspense, Ramon confronts his two greatest enemies in the waters of Baja California. The legendary curse of the Manta Diablo holds true when Ramon wrests the fabulous black pearl from the Manta's cave and his life is changed forever.

The Fearsome Inn   Isaac Bashevis Singer
Illustrated by Nonny Hogrogian   Scribner

> Unaware that the owners of the inn are a witch and her half-devil husband, three young men seek shelter there on a stormy winter night. One of the three, a clever student of the Cabala, recognizes the couple's evil and courageously defeats them, sending the pair "behind the Mountains of Darkness where there is neither day nor night."

The Egypt Game   Zilpha Keatley Snyder
Illustrated by Alton Raible   Atheneum

> April and Melanie begin the Egypt game in the backyard of a slightly sinister curio shop. With costumes, ceremonies, an evil god, an oracular owl, and four other members, the game is seriously and imaginatively played. After the murder of a child, they are forced inside for awhile, but finally they begin the game again. This time one of the players almost becomes the next victim.

1967 AWARD

Up a Road Slowly   Irene Hunt   Follett

When Julie is seven, her mother dies. She and her little brother are sent to live with her strict, schoolteacher aunt. Through the years, Julie keeps hoping that her father will want them back, that staying with Aunt Cordelia is just temporary, but slowly she comes to love her aunt and wants to stay.

HONORS

The King's Fifth   Scott O'Dell
Illustrated by Samuel Bryant   Houghton

> Imprisoned in Vera Cruz and awaiting trial, seventeen-year-old Esteban tells of his part in the disastrous expedition for gold to the Seven Cities of Cibola. A map-maker, Esteban is left with the bags of gold. After seeing the greed, cruelty, and, finally, death of those searching for it, he throws the gold into a volcanic crater.

Zlateh the Goat and Other Stories   Isaac Bashevis Singer
Illustrated by Maurice Sendak   Harper

> Seven stories rich with eastern European culture and Jewish folklore are filled with lively characters, delightfully funny fools, clever people, and loyal animals. The ink drawings of Sendak create wonderful scenes complementing the stories perfectly.

The Jazz Man   Mary Hays Weik   Illustrated by Ann Grifalconi   Atheneum

> Night after night Zeke and his mother and father listen to the jazz man play his piano. Then his mother tires of his father not working, and she leaves them. Soon his father goes as well, and Zeke is alone. As the gloomy days and nights pass, Zeke dreams of the jazz man and of better, happier times.

1966 AWARD

I, Juan de Pareja   Elizabeth Borton de Trevino   Farrar

Behind the great painter Velasquez stands his faithful slave, Juan, ready to prepare a canvas, mix paint, and boost his morale. But, secretly, Juan teaches himself to paint, winning his freedom and the respect of a great master.

HONORS

The Black Cauldron   Lloyd Alexander   Holt

Assistant Pig-Keeper Taran excitedly joins Gwydion and the other men of Prydain in their attack on Arawn, Lord of Annuvin, and his cauldron-born army. Only by destroying the cauldron can they hope to stop Arawn and his deathless warriors from overrunning Prydain.

The Animal Family   Randall Jarrell   Illustrated by Maurice Sendak   Pantheon

Isolated in his house by the sea, the hunter is lonely until the day he sees the mermaid. Together they form an amazing family with first a bear cub, then a lynx, and finally an orphaned boy. Each fits gently and beautifully into the very special world created by the unusual couple.

The Noonday Friends   Mary Stolz   Illustrated by Louis Glanzman   Harper

Her hard-working mother and out-of-work father depend on Franny to take care of her little brother after school and to help out in other ways. The only time left for friendship is during lunch hour at school when she talks to Simone, a friend with whom she can share problems.

1965 AWARD

Shadow of a Bull   Maia Wojciechowska
Illustrated by Alvin Smith   Atheneum

With everyone waiting for him to become a great bullfighter like his father, Manolo is afraid to let them know that he has a different dream—to become a doctor. He trains and practices for the ring until finally he has the courage and confidence to admit that he can never be a bullfighter.

HONOR

Across Five Aprils   Irene Hunt   Follett

At nine, Jethro is excited by the prospect of a civil war coming to the country. When the nation really does go to war, his brothers and friends go in different directions, fighting for either the North or the South. Jethro begins to understand how devastating war really is to family and nation.

1964 AWARD

It's Like This, Cat   Emily Neville   Illustrated by Emil Weiss   Harper

When his father suggests that owning a dog might be good for him, fourteen-year-old Dave defiantly goes to Aunt Kate the Cat Woman and adopts a stray. The cat ends up leading him to new people and adventures all over Manhattan—and even to an appreciation for his parents.

HONORS

Rascal: A Memoir of a Better Era   Sterling North
Illustrated by John Schoenherr   Dutton

> For twelve months Sterling owned the raccoon, raising him from a tiny captured kit to a large adult yearning for his freedom. Bright, curious, energetic, and endearing, Rascal fills the boy's life with love, companionship, and adventure during their year together.

The Loner   Ester Wier   Illustrated by Christine Price   McKay

> Both nameless and homeless, the boy wanders the country with other migrants, hoping to find work and food. Finally, lost and weak from hunger, he collapses and is found by a woman called The Boss. The gruff but gentle sheep rancher names him David and gives him a chance to make his own life on her Montana ranch.

1963 AWARD

A Wrinkle in Time   Madeleine L'Engle   Farrar

Meg, Charles Wallace, and next-door neighbor Calvin go into space and through time to rescue Meg's father, a scientist who disappeared while working on a secret project. The children's intergalactic search leads them to a confrontation with the forces of evil on the planet Camazotz, where conformity means survival.

HONORS

Thistle and Thyme: Tales and Legends from Scotland   Sorche Nic Leodhas, pseud.
(Leclaire Alger)   Illustrated by Evaline Ness   Holt

> Using her memories of stories told in her family, the author retells ten stories based on Scottish legends and folktales. Some are humorous, others mysterious and suspenseful, and all of them possess the rhythm of the Gaelic language.

Men of Athens   Olivia Coolidge   Illustrated by Milton Johnson   Houghton

> The golden age of Greece comes to life through the men and women who lived during and immediately before and after that brief fifty-year period. The battles

they waged to make Greece strong and free; the brilliance of the leading artists, philosophers, and statesmen; and the excitement of the time make exciting reading.

1962 AWARD

The Bronze Bow   Elizabeth George Speare   Houghton

At the death of his parents, Daniel swears vengeance against the Roman invaders. For five years he hides in the mountains of Galilee with a band of rebels but finally must return to care for his sister. He meets Jesus but refuses to accept his message of love, wanting revenge instead. Only when all seems nearly lost does he start to understand the power of love.

HONORS

Frontier Living   Edwin Tunis   World

> Beginning with the settlement of the Piedmont area in the early 1700s, nineteen distinct frontier movements take American settlers from the East Coast across the continent and through the nineteenth century. Details of daily life and carefully drawn pictures of the people and objects show what makes this era unique.

The Golden Goblet   Eloise Jarvis McGraw   Coward

> Under the control of his cruel and unscrupulous half-brother, Gebu, Ranofer, a boy of ancient Egypt who lives in Thebes, is sent to work for a goldsmith. Slowly he discovers that Gebu is stealing gold objects from the Valley of the Tombs, and he must find a way to expose him.

Belling the Tiger   Mary Stolz   Illustrated by Beni Montresor   Harper

> Asa and Rambo, the two smallest mice, are given the dubious honor of belling the cat. While getting the bell, the two accidentally get stuck on a ship and travel to a tropical island where they "bell" a tiger. Home again, the diminutive duo have the courage to demand a raise in status.

1961 AWARD

Island of the Blue Dolphins   Scott O'Dell   Houghton

Accidentally left behind when her tribe flees, Karana spends eighteen years alone on an island off the coast of California. Her courage and resourcefulness help her to survive and to fill her life with moments of beauty and happiness.

HONORS

America Moves Forward: A History for Peter   Gerald W. Johnson
Illustrated by Leonard Everett Fisher   Morrow

> From World War I to 1956, major events and important men of politics are evaluated and discussed for their impact on American life and history. The third and final volume in a work that offers a personalized look at American history, the book is illustrated with striking scratchboard pictures.

Old Ramon   Jack Schaefer   Illustrated by Harold West   Houghton

> Old Ramon teaches the boy as much as he can during the months they spend with the sheep in the mountains. Along the way, Ramon shares stories of his youth as a shepherd with the boy's grandfather and brings the boy back to the valley with a keener understanding and appreciation for the life of a shepherd.

The Cricket in Times Square   George Selden, pseud. (George Thompson)
Illustrated by Garth Williams   Farrar

> Accidentally brought into a New York City subway station, Chester Cricket is found by Mario Bellini, the son of a newsstand owner. Chester is befriended by two subway animals, Harry Cat and Tucker Mouse, who encourage him to use his musical talents to help the Bellinis. An overnight success, Chester nonetheless longs to return to the country.

1960 AWARD

Onion John   Joseph Krumgold   Illustrated by Symeon Shimin   Crowell

Twelve-year-old Andy is torn between his love for his father and his affection for Onion John, the old man whose way of life is totally foreign to nearly everyone in town. When members of the Rotary Club try to build Onion John a new house, their actions have great repercussions.

HONORS

My Side of the Mountain   Jean Craighead George   Dutton

> Tired of living in a crowded city apartment, Sam Gribley runs away from home and heads for his Grandpa Gribley's long-lost homestead in the Catskill mountains. For a year he stays alone, learning to live off the land, hollowing out a tree for a home, taming a falcon, and using every bit of ingenuity and resourcefulness he has to survive.

America Is Born: A History for Peter   Gerald W. Johnson
Illustrated by Leonard Everett Fisher   Morrow

Johnson's account of America's history is a very personal retelling of the lives and adventures of the people who explored and settled this country. The first in a three-volume series, the book covers the time from Columbus to the Revolutionary War and the Constitutional Convention.

The Gammage Cup   Carol Kendall   Illustrated by Erik Blegvad   Harcourt

Five misfits are sent into exile in the mountains when they refuse to conform to Minnepin traditions of dress, ideas, and life-style. They come to the rescue of the Land Between the Mountains when they uncover an invasion plot by the Mushroom People.

1959 AWARD

The Witch of Blackbird Pond   Elizabeth George Speare   Houghton

When her grandfather dies, sixteen-year-old Kit leaves the West Indies to live with her Puritan Aunt Rachel and her family. Kit's lively personality, her bright clothes, and her friendship with an outcast Quaker woman make her a target for charges of witchcraft in 1687 New England.

HONORS

The Family under the Bridge   Natalie S. Carlson
Illustrated by Garth Williams   Harper

Armand, who wanders the streets of Paris without a care, finds that his place beneath a bridge has been invaded by three children and their mother. Though he does not want to have anything to do with the children, the old man soon becomes a grandfather figure to the family, helping them, sharing the fun of the city, and ultimately making them his responsibility.

Along Came a Dog   Meindert DeJong   Illustrated by Maurice Sendak   Harper

When her frostbitten toes fall off, the little red hen becomes a target for the other chickens' abuse. Only the big, homeless dog comes to her rescue, looking on her as something to guard and love as he tries to make the farm his home.

Chucaro: Wild Pony of the Pampa   Francis Kalnay
Illustrated by Julian de Miskey   Harcourt

Once wild on the Argentine pampa, Chucaro is captured and tamed by Pedrito and his gaucho friend Juan. When the patron demands a gentle horse for his spoiled and cruel son, it is Chucaro he gets in spite of Pedrito's determination to keep him.

The Perilous Road   William O. Steele   Illustrated by Paul Galdone   Harcourt

Eleven-year-old Chris passionately hates the Yankees invading his Tennessee homeland and wants to do anything to help the South. He is deaf to his father's words when he says war is the worst thing that can happen to people. Then Chris is caught in the middle of a savage battle and realizes how horrible war really is.

1958 AWARD

Rifles for Watie   Harold Keith   Crowell

Sixteen-year-old Jeff, already a combat veteran in the Union Army and winner of the Congressional Medal of Honor, is captured by the rebel troops of General Stand Watie, a Cherokee Indian, and forced to become one of his scouts.

HONORS

Gone-Away Lake   Elizabeth Enright
Illustrated by Beth and Joe Krush   Harcourt

All summer Julian and his ten-year-old cousin Portia explore the houses they discover around Gone-Away Lake. They tell no one about the place or the two old people living in one of the houses until a near tragedy exposes their secret.

Tom Paine, Freedom's Apostle   Leo Gurko   Illustrated by Fritz Kredel   Crowell

With hardly any education or money and only Ben Franklin's letter of introduction, Tom Paine goes to America and writes *Common Sense,* the first of his revolutionary pamphlets. The power and vision of Paine's writings and the violent feelings they aroused throughout his life are evident in this biography.

The Great Wheel   Robert Lawson   Viking

Aunt Honoria predicts that Conn will leave Ireland and head west. Now he is in Chicago working on a construction project for a man named Ferris. His aunt has also made the wild prediction that he will ride the world's biggest wheel. Conn does as soon as Mr. Ferris's daring project is completed for the Chicago World's Columbian Exposition of 1893.

The Horsecatcher   Mari Sandoz   Westminster

Unlike the other Cheyenne boys, Young Elk refuses to kill. He wants to capture and tame the wild horses of the prairie. When his father insists he join in their war, he runs away, returning months later with fifteen horses and the start of what becomes a nearly legendary way with wild horses.

1957 AWARD

Miracles on Maple Hill   Virginia Sorensen
Illustrated by Beth and Joe Krush   Harcourt

When her father finally returns from being a prisoner of war, Marley's family decides to try to make a new beginning on a beautiful farm in Pennsylvania. During their first year there, they marvel at the miracle of the sap rising in the maple trees and the changes in each other.

HONORS

Black Fox of Lorne   Marguerite de Angeli   Doubleday

Shipwrecked off the coast of medieval Scotland, identical twins Jan and Brus are the only ones left alive when their father and his men are murdered. They survive by tricking the Scots into thinking that only one of them exists. Having sworn to avenge their father's murder, they foil the man's treasonous plot and keep their vow.

The House of Sixty Fathers   Meindert DeJong
Illustrated by Maurice Sendak   Harper

Alone in his family sampan, Tien Pao lands in Japanese-occupied China and begins a dangerous journey back to Hengyang during World War II. On his way, a company of American airmen adopt him, and he finds himself with sixty strange but kind fathers who help him find his family.

Old Yeller   Fred Gipson   Illustrated by Carl Burger   Harper

Left to help care for the homestead while his father takes their cattle to Kansas, fourteen-year-old Travis initially resents the intrusion of the big yellow dog. The dog proves his worth by rescuing little Arliss from a bear and Travis from wild hogs, guaranteeing himself a home.

Mr. Justice Holmes   Clara Ingram Judson
Illustrated by Robert Todd   Follett

The son of a famous writer, Oliver Wendell Holmes Jr. is a daydreamer whose brilliance is not always apparent to his family. After serving in the Civil War, he becomes a lawyer and a teacher, trying to make law interesting and clear to those entering the profession. Well-respected but never wealthy, he becomes one of the country's most highly esteemed Supreme Court justices.

The Corn Grows Ripe   Dorothy Rhoads   Illustrated by Jean Charlot   Viking

A happy but often irresponsible twelve-year-old Yucatan boy must suddenly grow up when his father is injured. Tigre bravely goes to another village to get a bone-setter and then sets about clearing and burning the family's new corn field, a rit-ualized duty that goes back to Mayan times. He proves he can be reliable.

1956 AWARD

Carry On, Mr. Bowditch   Jean Lee Latham
Illustrated by John O'Hara Cosgrove   Houghton

In spite of having little education, Nat Bowditch manages to teach himself mathematics and the principles of navigation. When he gets the chance to sail as a second mate, he teaches the rest of the crew to navigate and even finds mistakes in the navigational tables. He later rewrites the tables, and they become a standard navigational tool.

HONORS

The Golden Name Day   Jennie Lindquist
Illustrated by Garth Williams   Harper

Staying with her Swedish-American grandparents while her mother is hospitalized, Nancy is warmly welcomed into an extended family of aunts, uncles, and cousins. With everyone else having a special Swedish Name Day to celebrate, the family unsuccessfully tries to find a matching Swedish name for Nancy. Only when a new family moves in is Nancy's problem solved.

The Secret River   Marjorie Kinnan Rawlings
Illustrated by Leonard Weisgard   Scribner

When hard times come to the Florida forest people, little Calpurnia and her dog, Buggyhorse, go to the wise woman of the forest for help. Advised to follow her nose, Calpurnia discovers a beautiful river full of fish. She catches many and brings them home, making hard times "soft."

Men, Microscopes, and Living Things   Katherine Shippen
Illustrated by Anthony Ravielli   Viking

The author begins with Aristotle and his investigation of natural science, then moves on to Pliny, Harvey, Linnaeus, Lamarck, and others. The lively yet factual writing provides interesting insights into the work of significant biologists.

1955 AWARD

The Wheel on the School   Meindert DeJong
Illustrated by Maurice Sendak   Harper

Inspired by Lina's composition about storks, her classmates and teacher decide to find a way to bring the birds and their luck back to their little Dutch village. As the children involve the people of the village in the search for a wheel and for a way to attach it to their school, they bring their small community together.

HONORS

Courage of Sarah Noble   Alice Dalgliesh
Illustrated by Leonard Weisgard   Scribner

> "Keep up your courage," Sarah's mother tells her when she leaves with her father to build a home in the wilderness. The home finished, Sarah stays with friendly Indians while her father goes back for the rest of the family.

Banner in the Sky   James Ullman   Lippincott

> Although his father died trying to climb the Citadel, the highest mountain in the Alps, Rudy is determined to scale it himself. He hides his climbing ability from his mother and his Alpine-guide uncle and joins an English expedition hoping to be able to plant his father's red shirt at the top as a banner in the sky.

1954 AWARD

. . . And Now Miguel   Joseph Krumgold
Illustrated by Jean Charlot   Crowell

Every spring Miguel hopes this is the year he will be asked to join the men as they take their sheep up into the Sangre de Cristo Mountains of New Mexico. When at the age of twelve he is told it is not yet time for him, he works hard and prays that his father will see how grown up he is.

HONORS

All Alone   Claire Huchet Bishop
Illustrated by Feodor Rojankovsky   Viking

> When his father sends him to the high pastures with the heifers, Marcel is forcefully reminded of the village motto, "Each man for himself." But loneliness makes the yodel of another boy welcome, and when disaster strikes, Marcel is saved by his willingness to help someone else.

Magic Maize   Mary and Conrad Buff   Illustrated by the authors   Houghton

With the gringo world encroaching on the old ways of the Indians of Guatemala, a father continues to teach his son the old ways of farming and of praying to the gods of planting and harvest. Yet when their crop fails, it is the gringos who come to the family's aid.

Hurry Home, Candy   Meindert DeJong   Illustrated by Maurice Sendak   Harper

Taken from his mother before he is weaned and given to a family that only knows how to hurt and control him, Candy is lost on a family outing and becomes a stray. He longs for his own home and for people who will really love him.

Shadrach   Meindert DeJong   Illustrated by Maurice Sendak   Harper

After Davie's grandfather promises him a rabbit of his own, the little boy's excitement is nearly uncontainable. Davie bravely gathers food near a dangerous Dutch canal, helps get his hutch ready, and, when the rabbit arrives, lavishes attention and affection on the little animal.

Theodore Roosevelt, Fighting Patriot   Clara Ingram Judson
Illustrated by Lorence F. Bjorklund   Follett

Independent and honorable, Theodore is forever facing challenges because of his poor health, bad vision, and determination to learn as much as he can. As an adult he is remembered for leading the Rough Riders up San Juan Hill, starting our national park system, and being a president with tremendous courage and integrity.

1953 AWARD

Secret of the Andes   Ann Nolan Clark
Illustrated by Jean Charlot   Viking

Determined to discover another way of life, Cusi leaves his beautiful Incan home in the Andes Mountains and goes to the lowlands of Spanish Peru. Once there he longs for the hidden valley and the Old One. He returns knowing that he will never again willingly leave his home or break his vow to keep the Incan secret.

HONORS

The Bears on Hemlock Mountain   Alice Dalgliesh
Illustrated by Helen Sewell   Scribner

"There are no bears on Hemlock Mountain, no bears at all," Jonathan repeats as he goes over the mountain to borrow the big iron pot. But on the way back, Jonathan learns that there are indeed bears on Hemlock Mountain.

Birthdays of Freedom, Vol. I   Genevieve Foster   Scribner

> Starting with the excitement of the signing of the Declaration of Independence, the author sweeps back in time to the cave dwellers. From that time to the fall of Rome in 476 A.D., the determination to gain freedom is shown as the spark that encourages great inventions, discoveries, and political movements.

Moccasin Trail   Eloise Jarvis McGraw   Illustrated by Paul Galdone   Coward

> A runaway who is clawed by a grizzly and left for dead, Jim is raised by the Crow Indians and becomes a mountain man. Receiving a letter from his little brother asking for help, Jim finds his orphaned family on a wagon train heading to Oregon. He agrees to stay with them on the dangerous journey west. It is Jim's courage and Crow training that help them survive.

Red Sails to Capri   Ann Weil   Illustrated by C. B. Falls   Viking

> Three wealthy strangers come to Michele's small island village and stay at his parents' inn. Their good spirits and desire for adventure soon convince Michele and his friends to help the strangers explore a forbidden cave. Their discovery of the now-famous Blue Grotto changes the lives of everyone on Capri.

Charlotte's Web   E. B. White   Illustrated by Garth Williams   Harper

> After being raised by the farmer's daughter, Wilbur, a pig, is sold to another farm where his companion is a gray spider named Charlotte. When it becomes apparent that Wilbur is being fattened up for slaughtering, Charlotte promises to save him. The words that begin appearing in Charlotte's web amaze the farmer and bring hope to Wilbur.

1952 AWARD

Ginger Pye   Eleanor Estes   Harcourt

The only clue to the mysterious disappearance of Ginger, the Pye family dog, is the unusual man in the mustard-colored hat. Jerry and Rachel look everywhere for their little dog, occasionally seeing the mustard-hatted man, and finally solve the mystery of Ginger's disappearance.

HONORS

Americans before Columbus   Elizabeth Baity   Illustrated by C. B. Falls   Viking

> A study of pre-Columbian peoples in the Americas, this book describes their art, architecture, music, literature, and culture from the earliest times to that of Columbus. The text is prefaced with photographs of art and architecture and includes ink drawings in every chapter.

The Apple and the Arrow   Mary and Conrad Buff   Houghton

Caught by tyrant Gessler's soldier, Walter's father, William Tell, is forced to either shoot an apple on Walter's head or die. He successfully shoots the apple but is imprisoned. Breaking free, Tell kills Gessler and starts the revolution that wins Switzerland's freedom.

Minn of the Mississippi   Holling C. Holling   Houghton

Over a twenty-five-year period a snapping turtle makes her way from the source of the Mississippi to the Delta. Along the way she encounters a variety of adventures, lays eggs as she grows older, and introduces readers to the varied people, places, and wildlife along the river.

The Defender   Nicholas Kalashnikoff
Illustrated by Claire and George Louden   Scribner

In turn-of-the-century Siberia, Turgen, a widowed hunter and herbalist, becomes the target of the local shaman when he begins to protect the shy, fast-disappearing mountain rams. Turgen's only friends are a poor widow, whom he befriends and marries, and her two children.

The Light at Tern Rock   Julia L. Sauer   Illustrated by Georges Schreiber   Viking

Although Mr. Flagg has promised to get them back to shore by December 15, Aunt Martha and Ronnie suddenly realize that they are stuck at the lonely lighthouse until after Christmas. At first angry and sullen, Ronnie finally joins Aunt Martha in a very special celebration of the holiday.

1951 AWARD

Amos Fortune, Free Man   Elizabeth Yates
Illustrated by Nora S. Unwin   Dutton

Captured by slavers, Amos, son of an African king, survives the long ocean voyage only to be sold to a New England Quaker. After years of serving and learning from others, Amos buys his own freedom, sets up his own business, and begins to buy and set free other slaves.

HONORS

Gandhi, Fighter without a Sword   Jeanette Eaton
Illustrated by Ralph Ray   Morrow

From an upper-class life in India, Gandhi travels to England where he becomes a lawyer. Later he goes to South Africa and becomes involved in fighting for civil liberties. Back in India, Gandhi spends the remainder of his life leading the non-violent independence movement, which finally brings freedom to India and martyrdom to Gandhi.

Better Known as Johnny Appleseed   Mabel Leigh Hunt
Illustrated by James Daugherty   Lippincott

Loved by the settlers and the Indians, John Chapman carves a new name and legend for himself by trekking through the wilderness planting apple trees and helping anyone in need. The few facts known about Chapman are carefully interwoven with the Johnny Appleseed legends.

Abraham Lincoln, Friend of the People   Clara Ingram Judson
Illustrated with drawings by Robert Frankenberg and Kodachromes
of the Chicago Historical Society Lincoln Dioramas   Follett

Vividly written and carefully researched, the book portrays the struggles Abraham Lincoln has in learning to read, making a living, and finally entering politics. The difficulties of life on the frontier and the problems leading to the Civil War form the background.

The Story of Appleby Capple   Anne Parrish   Harper

For his Cousin Clement's ninety-ninth birthday, five-year-old Appleby is determined to give the old man the thing he wants most to see: a zebra butterfly. The boy wanders through the alphabet looking for the butterfly. Ink illustrations work people and objects around all twenty-six letters.

1950 AWARD

The Door in the Wall   Marguerite de Angeli   Doubleday

Crippled by a strange disease, Robin is ready to give up since he knows he will never be a knight. Then the monks help him to find ways to gain strength and courage and ultimately to play an important role in saving his medieval city.

HONORS

Tree of Freedom   Rebecca Caudill
Illustrated by Dorothy B. Morse   Viking

During the American Revolution, the Venable family leaves North Carolina to seek new land and get away from British oppression. Their exciting month-long trek over the mountains to Kentucky starts them on the way to new freedom, symbolized by the apple tree, whose seeds have come with the family all the way from France.

The Blue Cat of Castle Town   Catherine Coblentz
Illustrated by Janice Holland   Longmans

> Born under a blue moon, the little kitten is destined to carry the river's song of beauty, peace, and contentment to the unhappy people of Castle Town, Vermont. They have exchanged beauty for money, no longer making things with honesty and unable to "sing their own songs."

George Washington   Genevieve Foster   Scribner

> Filled with interesting excerpts from letters and diaries, this animated portrayal of the first president of the United States tells of George Washington's childhood and his many challenges as surveyor, soldier, commander in chief, and president.

Song of the Pines: A Story of Norwegian Lumbering in Wisconsin
Walter and Marion Havighurst   Illustrated by Richard Floethe   Winston

> An orphan, fifteen-year-old Nils joins the Svendsen family and other Norwegian emigrants as they head toward America in the 1850s. They travel to Wisconsin where they stake out a claim for a farm. Nils, having found work in the lumber camps, creates his own business and future in America.

Kildee House   Rutherford Montgomery
Illustrated by Barbara Cooney   Doubleday

> Not used to talking or being around people, Jerome Kildee retires to a small house he builds atop a hill in the redwood forest of northern California. Through the animals he shelters and the young people he meets, Kildee's life and the lives of those he encounters become fuller and richer than he ever imagined.

1949 AWARD

King of the Wind   Marguerite Henry
Illustrated by Wesley Dennis   Rand McNally

Sure that the motherless Arabian colt is going to be a great racer, Agba, the Sultan's mute slaveboy, raises the animal and stays with it, even when the horse is sent to France. Times are hard for the two, and they are often treated cruelly, but Agba never gives up his belief in the horse that becomes the ancestor of the great Man o' War.

HONORS

Story of the Negro   Arna Bontemps   Illustrated by Raymond Lufkin   Knopf

> Beginning with the first slave ship to come to Jamestown, Bontemps celebrates the culture and accomplishments of black people throughout the world: from the cultural heritage of Africa to the artists, leaders, and momentous events that have shaped not only black but world culture as well.

My Father's Dragon Ruth S. Gannett
Illustrated by Ruth Chrisman Gannett Random House

> An old alley cat convinces the narrator's father to rescue a baby dragon being used as a ferry by the animals of far-away Wild Island. With chewing gum, toothpaste, lollipops, and ribbons, the little boy keeps lions and tigers from eating him as he tries to rescue the little dragon.

Seabird Holling C. Holling Houghton

> To help him while away the hours on the whaling ship, Ezra carves a mascot, Seabird, which becomes his constant companion as he journeys around the world and finally gets his own ship. For four generations Seabird brings companionship and luck to Ezra's family as they sail the sea.

Daughter of the Mountain Louise Rankin
Illustrated by Kurt Wiese Viking

> When Momo's beloved Lhasa terrier is stolen by a wool trader, the Tibetan girl follows him on a long and dangerous journey that takes her through the mountains into India and finally to Calcutta.

1948 AWARD

The Twenty-One Balloons William Pène du Bois Viking

Professor Sherman leaves San Francisco in one hot air balloon and three weeks later is found in the Atlantic Ocean, clinging to the remains of twenty balloons and refusing to tell how he got there.

HONORS

The Quaint and Curious Quest of Johnny Longfoot Catherine Besterman
Illustrated by Warren Chappell Bobbs-Merrill

> Sent to the country to stay with his very thrifty uncle, Johnny, son of the shoe king, outwits guard dogs and a bear to reach the miserly old man. Not welcome, he goes on a quest that leads him to a cat who sends him to look for gold and seven-league boots. Leading a band of dogs, cats, bears, and his tagalong uncle, Johnny resourcefully succeeds in his mission.

Pancakes-Paris Claire Huchet Bishop
Illustrated by Georges Schreiber Viking

> Before the war there was heat and food and paper. Now Charles wishes for a way to show his little sister the fun of Mardi Gras and the wonderful crepes they ate. When two American soldiers suddenly enter his life and give him a strange box that they claim holds the ingredients for crepes, things start to happen.

The Cow-tail Switch, and Other West African Stories   Harold Courlander
Illustrated by Madye Lee Chastain   Holt

> Puns, trickster tales, creation tales, parables, and proverbs form the basis for these
> seventeen stories from West Africa. Faithfully retold from original sources, the
> stories are great fun to read or tell.

Li Lun, Lad of Courage   Carolyn Treffinger
Illustrated by Kurt Wiese   Abingdon

> When Li Lun refuses to join his father on his trip out to sea, the man angrily sends
> the boy up to the top of their mountain to grow rice. Alone on the mountaintop
> for 120 days, Li Lun, called a coward by his father and the other boys, coura-
> geously faces the elements, determined to complete his task.

Misty of Chincoteague   Marguerite Henry
Illustrated by Wesley Dennis   Rand McNally

> When Pony Penning Day comes on Chincoteague Island, Maureen and Paul are
> determined to buy the Phantom and her filly, Misty. They work hard and save
> $102, and finally the two spirited animals are theirs. Now the children must train
> the wild ponies to be around people, instead of running wild on Assateague.

1947 AWARD

Miss Hickory   Carolyn Sherwin Bailey
Illustrated by Ruth Gannett   Viking

With an apple twig for a body and a hickory nut for a head, Miss Hickory stubbornly
refuses help as she tries to survive a cold New Hampshire winter alone.

HONORS

Wonderful Year   Nancy Barnes   Illustrated by Kate Seredy   Messner

> Eleven-year-old Ellen and her fun-loving parents move from an easy life in
> Kansas to a ranch in western Colorado. They enjoy life as they plant trees and
> build a home and a barn. For Ellen, the best part is her friendship with fifteen-
> year-old Ronnie and the adventures they share.

Big Tree   Mary and Conrad Buff   Viking

> A glorious tree that can live thousands of years and has no fear of fire or insects,
> the redwood Wawona begins to grow long before the pyramids and the coming
> of Christ. Nothing threatens the huge and ancient tree until man arrives with axes
> and saws. But others recognize his importance and offer protection to the red-
> wood.

The Avion My Uncle Flew   Cyrus Fisher, pseud. (Darwin L. Teilhet)
Illustrated by Richard Floethe   Appleton

> When John's father returns home after World War II, he decides to take his wife and son to France. There John will have a chance to get his injured leg treated and to see his mother's homeland. John does not want to go, but he has no choice. Once there he becomes involved in a mysterious adventure that takes him to southern France and his glider-building uncle.

The Heavenly Tenants   William Maxwell   Illustrated by Ilonka Karasz   Harper

> The night before the Maxwells are to leave for three weeks in Virginia, father takes the children outside and shows them the different constellations that make up the zodiac. When no one comes to care for their animals while they are gone, the signs of the zodiac come to Earth and do it for them.

The Hidden Treasure of Glaston   Eleanore Jewett
Illustrated by Frederick T. Chapman   Viking

> When he is forced to leave the country because of his part in the murder of Thomas à Becket, Sir Hugh de Morville leaves his crippled son in the care of the monks at Glaston. As the boy and a new friend explore the area, they discover treasure left by King Arthur and his court and begin an exciting and suspenseful search for the Holy Grail.

1946 AWARD

Strawberry Girl   Lois Lenski   Lippincott

Birdie's family wants to make a good living growing strawberries and oranges in turn-of-the-century Florida. Unfortunately their shiftless neighbors, the Slaters, fight them every step of the way.

HONORS

Justin Morgan Had a Horse   Marguerite Henry
Illustrated by Wesley Dennis   Rand McNally

> Justin Morgan does not want the little colt that follows him and Joel home. But Joel raises and trains it, and the two soon realize that the little horse is something very special, not to mention very fast. Years later it becomes the first of a new breed: the Justin Morgan horse.

The Moved-Outers   Florence Crannell Means
Illustrated by Helen Blair   Houghton

> After the attack on Pearl Harbor, the Ohara family, who have always thought of themselves as Americans, are suddenly "Japanese." Put into internment camps

with only the barest of necessities, Sue and her family try not only to survive but to stay loyal Americans.

New Found World   Katherine Shippen   Illustrated by C. B. Falls   Viking

A history of Latin America, the book begins with a chapter on the topography and the plant and animal life of the area. Additional chapters discuss the native peoples and their interaction with European explorers and colonists. Well-researched, the book covers aspects of Latin American life and history up to the end of World War II.

Bhimsa, the Dancing Bear   Christine Weston
Illustrated by Roger Duvoisin   Scribner

While aimlessly walking in his Indian garden, David is surprised by the approach of a boy, Gopala, and his tame bear, Bhimsa. He eagerly runs away with the two as they wander through India trying to find a way home for Gopala. Bhimsa's dancing attracts attention everywhere, earning them food and getting them into and out of trouble along the way.

1945 AWARD

Rabbit Hill   Robert Lawson   Viking

The excitement among the wild creatures is contagious as Little Georgie enthusiastically tells every one of them that new folks are coming to the old farmhouse. All of the animals anxiously await the day the newcomers will arrive, afraid they might be the kind who have guns or dogs or even poison.

HONORS

The Silver Pencil   Alice Dalgliesh   Illustrated by Katherine Milhous   Scribner

After her father's sudden death, Janet and her mother begin a series of moves that take them from Trinidad, to England, to the United States, and then to Nova Scotia. Along the way, Janet holds fast to the silver pencil her father gave her, finding that writing is a solace.

Lone Journey: The Life of Roger Williams   Jeanette Eaton
Illustrated by Woodi Ishmael   Harcourt

From childhood onward, Roger Williams is a champion for religious freedom. Again and again he speaks out for separation of church and state, risking his own life and trying to save the lives of others. Finally Williams becomes the founder of the Providence Colony in America, where settlers of all religious faiths can find refuge.

The Hundred Dresses   Eleanor Estes
Illustrated by Louis Slobodkin   Harcourt

> Wanda Petronski, who speaks in broken English and always wears the same
> sparkling clean dress to school each day, brags to the other girls that she has a
> hundred dresses at home. Wanda is laughed at and teased by the other girls, and
> she and her family move away. Only then do the girls find Wanda's beautifully
> drawn pictures of one hundred dresses.

Abraham Lincoln's World   Genevieve Foster   Scribner

> As Abraham Lincoln grows from birth to death, the things happening through-
> out the world affect him and his country. Chapter by chapter the stories of not
> only Lincoln but also Napolean, Jefferson, Tecumseh, Jackson, Bismarck, and oth-
> ers are told alternately to give a full and fascinating picture of world events.

1944 AWARD

Johnny Tremain   Esther Forbes   Illustrated by Lynd Ward   Houghton

Fourteen-year-old apprentice silversmith Johnny Tremain has a terrible accident
that forces him to give up his work. He becomes involved with Sam Adams and the
other Boston patriots, takes part in the Boston Tea Party, and plays a role in the battle of Lexington.

HONORS

Rufus M.   Eleanor Estes   Illustrated by Louis Slobodkin   Harcourt

> A lively and imaginative little boy, Rufus is the youngest of the four Moffat chil-
> dren. Anxious to do his part for the war effort, he knits washcloths, plants a victo-
> ry garden, and earns enough money selling popcorn to become a Victory Boy.

Fog Magic   Julia Sauer   Illustrated by Lynd Ward   Viking

> In every generation of Addingtons there is one person for whom the dense fog of
> Nova Scotia is magical. Walking toward the deserted village of Blue Cove on a
> foggy day, Greta comes upon a thriving village she has never seen before. It is the
> Blue Cove of one hundred years ago.

These Happy Golden Years   Laura Ingalls Wilder
Illustrated by Helen Sewell and Mildred Boyle   Harper

> Laura Ingalls, though still a student herself, begins teaching in small schools and
> sewing to earn tuition money for Mary's education. Whether working hard in
> town, teaching, living on her family's claim on the Dakota prairie, or finally
> deciding to marry Almanzo, Laura realizes how lucky she is to have her warm,
> happy family.

Mountain Born   Elizabeth Yates   Illustrated by Nora S. Unwin   Coward

Nursed back to life by Peter's mother, Biddy, a black lamb, is given to six-year-old Peter to raise. Bright and brave, Biddy becomes the leader of the herd, repeatedly alerting her human keepers to impending disaster.

1943 AWARD

Adam of the Road   Elizabeth Janet Gray
Illustrated by Robert Lawson   Viking

Adam, his minstrel father, their horse, and Adam's trained dog, Nick, are traveling in thirteenth-century England, singing and telling stories for food and a place to sleep. When Nick is stolen, father and son try desperately to find him and become separated from each other.

HONORS

The Middle Moffat   Eleanor Estes   Illustrated by Louis Slobodkin   Harcourt

Janey is the "middle Moffat," trying hard to be serious and to do everything well. Things do not seem to work out quite as she plans (her organ recital turns into an escape for thousands of moths), but the little girl is undeterred. She continues to make bold plans with outrageously funny results.

"Have You Seen Tom Thumb?"   Mabel Leigh Hunt
Illustrated by Fritz Eichenberg   Lippincott

From the age of five, Charles Sherwood Stratton, only twenty-five inches tall and weighing fifteen pounds, is presented to the world by P. T. Barnum as General Tom Thumb. A charming, humorous person, he travels all over the world with Barnum.

1942 AWARD

The Matchlock Gun   Walter Edmonds   Illustrated by Paul Lantz   Dodd

Edward, his mother, and his little sister have only one defense against the French and the Indians—a huge matchlock gun. When attacked, his mother is wounded, and Edward must use the gun to save their lives.

HONORS

George Washington's World   Genevieve Foster   Scribner

From birth to death, the story of George Washington's life and the lives of other well-known kings, soldiers, politicians, and scientists of the same period are interwoven. In each section the author skillfully provides a worldview of events.

Down Ryton Water   Eva Roe Gaggin   Illustrated by Elmer Hader   Viking

Escaping the religious persecution of their English countrymen, Matt and his family and neighbors head down Ryton Water for freedom in Holland. Finally ready to face the long and dangerous voyage to the New World, all of them board the Mayflower and Speedwell to sail to what becomes the Plymouth Colony.

Indian Captive: The Story of Mary Jemison   Lois Lenski   Lippincott

Even though other settlers have been slaughtered by the French and the Indians, Pa refuses to let his family go east to safety. They, too, are captured, and only young, blond-haired Mary survives, forced to become a part of the Seneca people.

Little Town on the Prairie   Laura Ingalls Wilder
Illustrated by Helen Sewell and Mildred Boyle   Harper

Laura is fifteen and, in warm weather, working hard with Ma and Pa on their Dakota Territory claim. She earns what she can to help pay for Mary's courses at the College for the Blind, and, with her family, she spends the long, cold, but friend-filled winters in town.

1941 AWARD

Call It Courage   Armstrong Sperry   Macmillan

Mocked by the other boys because of his fear of the sea, Mafatu secretly takes a small boat and leaves his village. Alone on a terrifying ocean voyage, the boy, son of a Polynesian chief, overcomes his fear of the sea.

HONORS

Young Mac of Fort Vancouver   Mary Jane Carr
Illustrated by Richard Holberg   Crowell

Traveling west to Fort Vancouver in 1832, Young Mac is determined to become a fur-trading Northman and not a full-fledged member of the white world. Contact with Dr. McLoughlan, head of the fort, and other white and mixed-heritage men causes him to reconsider his decision.

Blue Willow   Doris Gates   Illustrated by Paul Lantz   Viking

With her small family wandering from place to place so that Dad can find work, Janey has never really had a home or school or friends. Maybe the San Joaquin Valley will be the place where everything changes, a place where they can stay and she can finally bring the blue willow plate out for good.

Nansen   Anna Gertrude Hall   Illustrated by Boris Artzybasheff   Viking

Determined to learn as much as he can as a little boy (and even more determined as an adult), Fridtjof Nansen grows to be one of Norway's most famous citizens.

He is an explorer who travels all the way to the North Pole, a statesman, and, most difficult of all, a fighter for world peace and a winner of the Nobel Peace Prize.

The Long Winter Laura Ingalls Wilder Illustrated by Helen Sewell and Mildred Boyle Harper

The Ingalls family, pioneering in the Dakota Territory, stoically endure a dreary succession of blizzards. Huddled in the family store, they and their neighbors must depend upon their ingenuity to prevent freezing and starvation.

1940 AWARD

Daniel Boone James Daugherty Viking

A rugged frontiersman and a leader of pioneers, Daniel Boone starts life in Pennsylvania and ends it eighty-six years later in Missouri, an almost legendary character. Boone's longing for adventure, his bravery, and his foolishness are examined honestly in this biography that sings the praises of pioneer men and women in words and vigorous drawings.

HONORS

Boy with a Pack Stephen W. Meader
Illustrated by Edward Shenton Harcourt

Bill fills a backpack with things to sell in Ohio and, with two years of savings, leaves his New Hampshire mill town on foot. The 1837 journey is long and hard but filled with all kinds of adventures, danger, and amazing good luck.

Runner of the Mountain Tops: The Life of Louis Agassiz Mabel Robinson
Illustrated by Lynd Ward Random House

A brilliant naturalist and the founder of Harvard's Agassiz Museum, Louis Agassiz is realistically portrayed from his childhood in Switzerland through his years as a Harvard professor. Agassiz's fascination with all of nature and his great teaching ability are evident throughout the book.

The Singing Tree Kate Seredy Viking

Four years after the end of *The Good Master,* the First World War has started, and Mother, Jancsi, and cousin Kate are left to take care of the farm as Father and Uncle Sandor are called to fight. The three of them hold the farm together and make it a refuge for orphans, relatives, and even prisoners of war.

By the Shores of Silver Lake Laura Ingalls Wilder
Illustrated by Helen Sewell and Mildred Boyle Harper

The Ingalls have not had a good crop since the grasshoppers came. Pa decides they will make one more move, this time to Dakota Territory. The family spends a happy winter taking in other settlers and earning money to send Mary, blind from scarlet fever, to a special school.

1939 AWARD

Thimble Summer   Elizabeth Enright   Farrar & Rinehart

All kinds of good things seem to happen after Garnet finds the silver thimble in the dried-up river bed. The nine-year-old farm girl notices that the drought finally breaks, she has an exciting time being locked in the public library with a friend, and her pet pig wins a blue ribbon at the fair.

HONORS

Nino   Valenti Angelo   Viking

While his father works in America to earn their fare to California, Nino and his mother stay with his grandfather in his small Italian village. The little boy and his family and friends share holidays, trips to the city, and small but exciting adventures that create a memorable picture of turn-of-the-century Italy.

Mr. Popper's Penguins   Richard and Florence Atwater
Illustrated by Robert Lawson   Little, Brown

From the moment he is given a penguin as a pet, Mr. Popper's life starts changing. He converts his basement into an ice rink, finds a friend for his lonely bird, and suddenly has twelve penguins to feed instead of one.

"Hello the Boat!"   Phyllis Crawford   Illustrated by Edward Laning   Holt

The entire Doak family pitches in to get their store-boat from Pittsburgh to Cincinnati in 1817. Along the Ohio River, settlers shout out, "Hello the boat!" and the family eagerly pushes the boat ashore and enthusiastically opens the store. On their way, the Doaks encounter thieves, learn about the history of the river area, and have a surprisingly good time.

Leader by Destiny: George Washington, Man and Patriot   Jeanette Eaton
Illustrated by Jack Manley Rose   Harcourt

Not a man who plans what he wants but rather one who allows things to shape him and his future, George Washington lives a life full of adventure and responsibility as he grows up. The fifty-two years of his life that Eaton covers contain much of the history and many of the famous people of his time.

Penn   Elizabeth Janet Gray   Illustrated by George Gillett Whitney   Viking

Until he converts to the Quaker religion, William Penn leads a privileged upper-class life. Then he loses everything and is imprisoned. After fighting hard for religious freedom, Penn is allowed to go to America and found the new colony of Pennsylvania, based on the principles for which he fought.

1938 AWARD

The White Stag   Kate Seredy   Viking

Based on legends about the founding of Hungary, this stirring story begins with Nimrod receiving a prophesy from God. He tells his people to follow the White Stag and Nimrod's sons to the west. During their long and dangerous journey, the people move valiantly westward until the birth of Attila, who one day leads them heroically into what becomes Hungary.

HONORS

Pecos Bill   James Cloyd Bowman
Illustrated by Laura Bannon   Little, Brown

> Raised by coyotes and able to speak to animals, Pecos Bill reluctantly accepts the knowledge that he is one of those dreaded inhuman humans. He becomes a cowboy and does things in legendary proportion: busting up a cyclone, breaking up a cattle rustling gang, and rounding up 39,000,000 cattle and driving them to market.

Bright Island   Mabel Robinson   Illustrated by Lynd Ward   Random House

> Strong, independent, and committed to life on her family's small island off the coast of Maine, Thankful very reluctantly agrees to attend school on the mainland. There, life is so foreign that she initially feels like a total outsider among the other high school students.

On the Banks of Plum Creek   Laura Ingalls Wilder
Illustrated by Helen Sewell and Mildred Boyle   Harper

> After finally reaching Minnesota and planting a wheat crop, the Ingalls lose it to a horde of grasshoppers. Determined to stay, Pa goes to work for other farmers. Laura goes to school, shares adventures with friends, but most of all enjoys the moments when her family is together and Pa is back playing the fiddle.

1937 AWARD

Roller Skates   Ruth Sawyer   Illustrated by Valenti Angelo   Viking

Her wealthy parents in Europe, Lucinda spends a glorious year living with two teachers, skating all over New York City, and making friends everywhere. The people she meets, whether it is her impoverished musician neighbor or the hansom cab driver, appreciate her energy, friendliness, and determination.

HONORS

The Golden Basket   Ludwig Bemelmans   Viking

A staid English father and his two little daughters visit Bruges, Belgium, and stay at the Golden Basket Hotel. The girls and the hotel owner's son enjoy exploring the famous city. While visiting a cathedral, they meet twelve little girls standing in two straight lines, the youngest and spunkiest being Madeline.

Winterbound   Margery Bianco   Viking

With both of their parents gone for months, nineteen-year-old Kay and sixteen-year-old Garry take on managing both the rented cottage and their younger brother and sister. During a long, cold, but very exciting depression-era winter, they make friends, earn and save money, and gain strength and independence.

The Codfish Musket   Agnes Hewes
Illustrated by Armstrong Sperry   Doubleday

Even as a youngster, Dan has a keen eye for fine rifles and arms. On a mission to Washington for his Boston employer, Dan becomes secretary to Thomas Jefferson. The president sends him into the frontier with a message for Merriwether Lewis, but along the way Dan spots gun thieves arming the Indians. He defeats them and delivers his message, finally returning to Washington.

Whistler's Van   Idwal Jones   Illustrated by Zhenya Gay   Viking

After his grandfather disappears one night with a cart and pony, Gwilyn decides he wants a chance to wander through Wales as well. When the Ringos, a family of gypsies, appear at the farmhouse and whistle, Gwilyn goes off with them for a summer full of music, adventure, and, most importantly, horses.

Phebe Fairchild: Her Book   Lois Lenski   Stokes

When Phebe's mother decides to join Phebe's father on a sea voyage, the ten-year-old is sent to stay with relatives in the country. Life in 1830 rural Connecticut at first seems rigid to Phebe, and her copy of *Mother Goose* is a constant source of support. The child comes to appreciate her relatives, their simple life, their generosity, and their sense of fun.

Audubon   Constance Rourke   Illustrated by James MacDonald   Harcourt

Despite mysterious beginnings, John James Audubon manages to leave France and go to America. He marries but continues to traipse the countryside in search of birds and small animals to paint. Carefully researched, the book offers a well-rounded look at the man who became known for his nineteenth-century paintings of American birds.

1936 AWARD

Caddie Woodlawn   Carol Ryrie Brink   Macmillan

Eleven years old in 1864, Caddie roams the woods and rivers of western Wisconsin with her brothers as her mother relentlessly tries to make her into a young "lady." The mischievous redhead's adventures with Indians and pioneers are full of fun and excitement.

HONORS

Young Walter Scott   Elizabeth Janet Gray   Viking

Despite years of living with country relatives, Walter is determined not to let his lame leg stand in his way once he is at home again. This lively, fictionalized biography transports readers to late eighteenth-century Edinburgh, Scotland, and offers an engrossing introduction to the life of the famous novelist.

The Good Master   Kate Seredy   Viking

Jancsi is fascinated by his city cousin Kate's daring and reckless behavior. Whether she is stopping a stampede of horses, nearly drowning in the river, or running off with gypsies, she is a marvel and a delight to the Hungarian country folk.

All Sail Set: A Romance of the Flying Cloud   Armstrong Sperry   Winston

Fifteen-year-old Thach goes to work for the great Donald McKay making drawings of his plans for the clipper ship *Flying Cloud*. The ship completed, Thach becomes an apprentice, sails around the Horn, is initiated by "Neptune," contends with mutineers, and nearly loses his life in a shipboard fire.

Honk, the Moose   Phil Stong   Illustrated by Kurt Wiese   Dodd

The temperature is thirty below zero and the snow is seven feet deep when the boys find a moose in Ivar's father's stable. The town is in an uproar as everyone tries to think of ways to get the gentle and very funny beast to leave.

1935 AWARD

Dobry   Monica Shannon   Illustrated by Atanas Katchamakoff   Viking

Bulgarian peasant boy Dobry tries to convince his mother that he must be an artist. He does not want to plow the fields as his ancestors did. Dobry's grandfather understands, but until Dobry sculpts a beautiful nativity scene in the snow to prove his talents, his mother is not convinced.

HONORS

Davy Crockett   Constance Rourke   Illustrated by James MacDonald   Harcourt

> Davy Crockett is a bigger-than-life character: he is a pioneer, hunter, teller of tales, soldier, statesman, and legendary American hero. Rourke writes a well-researched and well-documented biography filled with anecdotes and comments by Crockett and his contemporaries.

Pageant of Chinese History   Elizabeth Seeger
Illustrated by Bernard Watkins   Longmans

> Using a conversational style, Seeger leads the reader through Chinese history starting with mythical and legendary times. Then she writes about each of the dynasties, ending with the Manchu in 1912 and the beginning of the republic. Political and cultural history are the focus of most of the book.

A Day on Skates: The Story of a Dutch Picnic   Hilda Van Stockum   Harper

> The canals of Holland are finally frozen solid, and the headmaster has a surprise. He takes the children on an all-day skating picnic. In spite of a few accidents, it is a thoroughly enjoyable time. Many black-and-white drawings and eight full-color illustrations show the festive atmosphere of the day.

1934 AWARD

Invincible Louisa: The Story of the Author of Little Women
Cornelia Meigs   Little, Brown

The life of Louisa May Alcott is chronicled through her lively involvement with family and friends. Incidents reveal that her invincible spirit keeps the family afloat during the darkest of times and always keeps them happy. Family photographs and a chronology are included.

HONORS

The Winged Girl of Knossos   Erick Berry, pseud. (Allena Best)   Appleton

> Spirited, athletic, and beautiful Inas, daughter of Daidalos, helps her father with his flying experiments on the Isle of Crete during the time of King Minos. Having to leave Crete hurriedly, she does so by flying out on a glider built by her father.

The Big Tree of Bunlahy: Stories of My Own Countryside   Padraic Colum
Illustrated by Jack Yeats   Macmillan

> Twelve fine old Irish tales and one original one are woven together by the story-teller who introduces each story. All are said to have been heard under the Tree of

Bunlahy, the great elm tree with big, smooth stones under it. There the villagers would sit and listen to these tales of animals, heroes, and leprechans.

The ABC Bunny   Wanda Gág   Coward

Lithographs filled with curved lines show a bunny romping through his day. After being scared out of his bed by a crashing apple, the bunny meets many animals. Each large, bright red letter of the alphabet is accompanied by a text that carries the ABC lesson along in a rhythmic manner. The song, with words and music, is included.

Glory of the Seas   Agnes Hewes   Illustrated by N. C. Wyeth   Knopf

The exciting early days of the clipper ships, the controversial Fugitive Slave Law, and the inner conflict caused by civil disobedience are at the center of this story set in Boston in the 1850s. When the *Flying Cloud* sails to San Francisco in just eighty-nine days, many Bostonians dream of sailing to California.

The Apprentice of Florence   Anne Kyle
Illustrated by Erick Berry, pseud. (Allena Best)   Houghton

Nemo, a sixteen-year-old Florentine apprentice, is sent to Constantinople on business in 1453. The city is besieged by Turks, and Nemo is hurt. On his return, young Christopher Columbus tells him that his father, thought to be dead, is alive. More adventures ensue as Nemo searches for his lost father.

New Land   Sarah Schmidt   Illustrated by Frank Dobias   McBride

It is the 1930s when Dad, the seventeen-year-old twins, and their younger sister arrive in Wyoming to homestead on an unproved claim. Rivalries on the football field and in the new vocational school, a blinding snowstorm, and troubles with the "big man" are overcome, and a new home is established.

Swords of Steel   Elsie Singmaster   Illustrated by David Hendrickson   Houghton

Although he has heard talk of the differences between the North and the South, it is not until 1859, when his beloved, free black friend is kidnapped to be sold, that John feels personal involvement in the conflict. In six years John grows from childhood to manhood with the Civil War intruding on and then enveloping his life.

The Forgotten Daughter   Caroline Snedeker
Illustrated by Dorothy P. Lathrop   Doubleday

When his wife dies in childbirth while he is traveling, the Roman centurion is told that both mother and child are dead. His daughter is subjected to the hardships of second-century life as a slave. Eventually she falls in love with a high-born Roman and the plague unites her with her father.

1933 AWARD

Young Fu of the Upper Yangtze   Elizabeth Lewis
Illustrated by Kurt Wiese   Winston

The empress has died and political life is in turmoil when Young Fu and his mother move from their village to Chungking so that he can be apprenticed to a coppersmith. Young Fu must constantly use his wits to protect his mother and himself from thieves and rascals.

HONORS

Children of the Soil: A Story of Scandinavia   Nora Burglon
Illustrated by Edgar Parin d'Aulaire   Doubleday

Two very poor but ambitious and industrious children live with their mother in Sweden at the turn of the twentieth century. The soil they hoe is poor, their crab trap washes out to sea, and a weaving contest is lost to the gentry. With a little help from a Tomte and a lot of work on their part, they acquire some livestock and the promise of a happier future.

Swift Rivers   Cornelia Meigs
Illustrated by Forrest W. Orr   Little, Brown

When his mean-spirited uncle locks him out of the house where he was raised, Chris knows it is time to become a man. The harsh 1835 Wisconsin winter and the bountiful woods lead him to try floating logs down to St. Louis. As a part of the early days of the logging industry, Chris has many adventures on the river.

The Railroad to Freedom: A Story of the Civil War   Hildegarde Swift
Illustrated by James Daugherty   Harcourt

Harriet Tubman, a slave, escapes from the South but goes back again and again, leading three hundred other slaves North to freedom via the dangerous Underground Railroad. The horrifying yet often thrilling adventures are based on incidents from Tubman's life.

1932 AWARD

Waterless Mountain   Laura Adams Armer
Illustrated by Sidney and Laura Armer   Longmans

Destined to become a medicine man, introspective Younger Brother learns the songs and stories of the Navajo Indians and begins to create songs of his own. Skillfully interwoven into the story are the early twentieth-century culture and heritage of the tribe.

HONORS

Jane's Island   Marjorie Allee
Illustrated by Maitland de Gorgoza   Houghton

> Ellen, a college freshman, spends the summer with twelve-year-old Jane in Woods Hole, Massachusetts, where Jane's father is a marine biologist. The girls enjoy light summer adventures while fishing and picnicking. Jane is a competent naturalist who imparts a good measure of scientific information throughout the story.

Truce of the Wolf and Other Tales of Old Italy   Mary Gould Davis
Illustrated by Jay Van Everen   Harcourt

> Seven widely varied Italian stories tell of such things as Saint Francis taming a menacing wolf, of an obstinate and heroic donkey, and of how a street in Florence was named. The tales, all told with a bit of Italian folk humor, come from many sources, including a Tuscan peasant woman and *The Decameron*.

Calico Bush   Rachel Field   Illustrated by Allen Lewis   Macmillan

> In 1743, twelve-year-old Marguerite is bound out to a family in Maine. Discriminated against by the parents because she is French, she finds happiness with the children as they all face hardships and the rigors of life in the Maine wilderness.

The Fairy Circus   Dorothy P. Lathrop   Macmillan

> When the circus tent goes up, it is so big that it encloses the places where the fairies live. They all scramble for the best view, and when it is over they decide to have a circus of their own. The fairies and woodland animals use grand imaginations as they re-create the circus in their own way.

Out of the Flame   Eloise Lownsbery
Illustrated by Elizabeth Tyler Wolcott   Longmans

> In the sixteenth century, Pierre is first a page then a squire as he becomes trained to be a knight in the court of Francis I. He attends tournaments, visits with great intellectuals, and learns music and botany with the royal children. Before the story ends, he and the children are abducted and released by pirates.

Boy of the South Seas   Eunice Tietjens
Illustrated by Myrtle Sheldon   Coward-McCann

> When a ship arrives in the harbor of the Marquesas Islands, young Teiki's curiosity gets ahold of him, and he climbs aboard and falls asleep. He awakens when the vessel is under sail and there is no turning back. At the island of Moorea, he swims ashore and makes a new life for himself.

1931 AWARD

The Cat Who Went to Heaven   Elizabeth Coatsworth
Illustrated by Lynd Ward   Macmillan

A starving Japanese artist is commissioned to paint the death of Buddha. He longs to include his gentle cat, Good Fortune, among the animals, but legend says cats cannot enter heaven. Because of her goodness, he paints her, and the little animal dies of happiness. When the priest objects, the painting miraculously changes to show Buddha accepting the cat.

HONORS

Mountains Are Free   Julia Davis Adams
Illustrated by Theodore Nadejen   Dutton

Bruno, a young Swiss orphan who is being raised by the Tells, suddenly decides to become a page to an Austrian, saying he will return when he can earn his own way. The stirring of democracy causes conflicts as the Swiss try to rebel against the harshness of their Habsburg rulers.

Garram the Hunter: A Boy of the Hill Tribes   Herbert Best
Illustrated by Erick Berry, pseud. (Allena Best)   Doubleday

Hoping to find an ally for his chieftain father, Garram is sent to stay with the emir and becomes a favorite of the ruler. When he returns home, he discovers not only a plot to imprison his father but receives word that the eastern tribes are threatening.

Meggy MacIntosh   Elizabeth Janet Gray
Illustrated by Marguerite de Angeli   Doubleday

In 1775 orphaned fifteen-year-old Meggy leaves her native Scotland to sail for the colony of North Carolina. There she joins Flora MacDonald, who had helped Bonnie Prince Charlie escape. Meggy becomes involved in the revolutionary cause and moves away from Flora, a loyalist.

Spice and the Devil's Cave   Agnes Hewes   Illustrated by Lynd Ward   Knopf

At a workshop in Portugal, Bartholomew Diaz, Vasco da Gama, and Ferdinand Magellan gather to discuss their theory that an all-sea route around the Cape of Good Hope, also known as the Devil's Cave, must exist. The theft by pirates of the only known maps adds interest and intrigue.

Queer Person   Ralph Hubbard   Illustrated by Harold von Schmidt   Doubleday

He can neither hear nor talk, and at age four he wanders into a camp of Pikuni Indians. His silence earns him the name Queer Person, and he is raised by an old woman in the tribe. During his test of bravery, he rescues the chief's lost son from the Crows, and it is revealed that they are brothers.

Ood-Le-Uk the Wanderer   Alice Lide and Margaret Johansen
Illustrated by Raymond Lufkin   Little, Brown

> An Alaskan Eskimo caught on an ice floe crosses the Bering Straight. After years of wandering, he returns home to establish trade between his tribe and the Siberian tribesmen. Once known as a weakling, after his hazardous adventures he is known to be a brave man.

The Dark Star of Itzá: The Story of a Pagan Princess   Alida Malkus
Illustrated by Lowell Houser   Harcourt

> When the khan of Chichén Itzá kidnaps the betrothed of another Mayan chieftain, war breaks out, and the city falls into the hands of the Toltecs. The seventeen-year-old daughter of Chichén Itzá's chief priest agrees to be the sacrifice that will save her city, but her father bravely finds a way to save her.

Floating Island   Anne Parrish   Harper

> All packed up and on board a ship bound for the tropics, a doll family and their doll house land on Floating Island after their ship wrecks. They adapt well to the island but soon realize that dolls can never be happy if they are away from children for too long. They then arrange their own rescue.

1930 AWARD

Hitty, Her First Hundred Years   Rachel Field
Illustrated by Dorothy P. Lathrop   Macmillan

Carved from a block of mountain ash a hundred years before, the six-and-a-half-inch doll now sits secure in the antique shop window and writes her memoirs. She recounts the adventures she had with many different people in places around the world. Illustrations show Hitty in many styles of clothing in her life thus far.

HONORS

Vaino   Julia Davis Adams   Illustrated by Lempi Ostman   Dutton

> Ancient legends of Finland, the lives of three children, and the Finnish Revolution of 1917 are blended together to tell a story filled with strong patriotic spirit. Vaino and his older brother and sister become a part of the revolution that finally frees Finland of foreign domination.

A Daughter of the Seine: The Life of Madame Roland   Jeanette Eaton   Harper

Madame Roland's life coincides with the French Revolution. The historical biography describes the childhood, married life, and tragic execution by guillotine of this remarkable woman. Madame Roland is intelligent and strongly supports the revolution, and her salon is depicted as the headquarters of much political activity.

The Jumping-Off Place   Marian Hurd McNeely
Illustrated by William Siegel   Longmans

When the uncle who cared for them dies, four children pull up stakes in Wisconsin and move to South Dakota. There they weather adventures, hardships, and squatters for the fourteen months it takes to make homesteaders owners of the land.

Pran of Albania   Elizabeth Miller
Illustrated by Maud and Miska Petersham   Doubleday

In post-World War I Albania amidst a threat of attack from Slavs, fourteen-year-old Pran falls in love. Rather than submit to an arranged marriage, she vows to never marry. After a truce is made, Pran realizes the man she loves is the same man her parents had arranged for her to marry.

Little Blacknose   Hildegarde Swift   Illustrated by Lynd Ward   Harcourt

Little Blacknose is none other than the DeWitt Clinton Engine, the first locomotive built for the New York Central Railway. The personified engine tells of his life until he becomes enthroned in New York's Grand Central Terminal.

The Tangle-Coated Horse and Other Tales   Ella Young
Illustrated by Vera Bock   Longmans

The Fionn Saga, the stories of Finn McCool known in every Gaelic-speaking part of Scotland and all over Ireland, is retold with vigor. The stories begin when McCool is a small boy learning about his heritage and his crafts and end three hundred years later when his son returns from the country of the Ever-Young.

1929 AWARD

The Trumpeter of Krakow   Eric P. Kelly
Illustrated by Angela Pruszynska   Macmillan

For two hundred years the Charnetski family has guarded Poland's most famous jewel. When the czar of Russia finds out about the valuable crystal, he sends men to steal it before the Charnetskis can get it to the king of Poland. Adventure, mystery, and self-sacrifice fill this medieval story set in Krakow.

HONORS

The Pigtail of Ah Lee Ben Loo   John Bennett   Longmans

Many original stories in prose and verse, and one brief wordless story, are illustrated with two hundred intriguing and often funny silhouettes. The stories are filled with robust and irreverent humor: King Arthur's Sir Launcelot is called "Sir Launcelot de Id-i-otte"! Most of the stories first appeared in *St. Nicholas Magazine.*

Millions of Cats   Wanda Gág   Coward

A lonely old couple decides to get a cat. Searching for the prettiest one out of a whole hillside filled with cats, the man comes home with "hundreds of cats, thousands of cats, millions and billions and trillions of cats." When the cats fight about who is prettiest, only one is left.

The Boy Who Was   Grace Hallock
Illustrated by Harrie Wood   Dutton

In 1927 Nino the goatherd shows an artist the wooden figures he has carved of famous Mediterranean people and proceeds to tell their stories, covering more than 3,000 years of history. He begins with tales of Odysseus, Pompeii, and the Crusades and then goes through the nineteenth century, occasionally including himself in the stories.

Clearing Weather   Cornelia Meigs   Illustrated by Frank Dobias   Little, Brown

It is just after the American Revolution and the economy has not recovered. When young Nicholas Drury takes over his family's shipbuilding business, he struggles hard until the family fortune reverses itself with the successful design, construction, and voyage of the Jocasta, a forerunner of the clipper ship.

Runaway Papoose   Grace Moon   Illustrated by Carl Moon   Doubleday

Little Nah-tee runs away when outlaw Indians attack her family's camp. Her parents cannot find her and move on with the others. Nah-tee and a young shepherd boy she meets have many adventures as they cross the mesa in search of her parents.

Tod of the Fens   Elinor Whitney   Illustrated by Warwick Goble   Macmillan

Fifteenth-century Boston, England, is the setting for the amusing tale of Tod, who lives with a band of men just outside of town. Prince Hal, later to become Henry V, roves about the town in various disguises. Tod, realizing what is happening, tells no one and plays along with the game that is afoot.

1928 AWARD

Gay Neck, the Story of a Pigeon   Dhan Gopal Mukerji   Dutton

Born in Calcutta, Gay Neck has thrilling adventures, first traveling all over India and later working as a carrier pigeon for the Indian Army in France during World War I. Eventually he returns to his young owner in India. Sometimes the story is told by Mukerji and at other times by Gay Neck the pigeon.

HONORS

Downright Dencey   Caroline Snedeker
Illustrated by Maginel Wright Barney   Doubleday

A Nantucket Quaker community during the War of 1812 provides the background for the story of a young girl named Dencey who first becomes involved with outcast Sammie when she hurls a stone at him. Ashamed, she tries to make amends but Sammie's trust must be won, and that is not easy for Dencey.

The Wonder Smith and His Son   Ella Young
Illustrated by Boris Artzybasheff   Longmans

Fourteen stories of Gubbaun Saor, a mythological creature of Ireland, have been retold from tales the author heard from English and Gaelic storytellers. The stories capture the lilting cadence of the Irish language and are enhanced by the graphics.

1927 AWARD

Smoky, the Cowhorse   Will James   Scribner

Born free on the open range, Smoky roams the hills until he is caught and gentled by Clint, a cowboy. Stolen and cruelly treated, Smoky kills his captor and runs as an outlaw. Captured again, he becomes a rodeo horse until once more he meets up with Clint and lives out his life on the range where he was born.

HONOR

No record.

1926 AWARD

Shen of the Sea   Arthur Bowie Chrisman
Illustrated by Else Hasselriis   Dutton

Sixteen charming and funny original stories are told in traditional folktale style. Most of the stories explain the origins of things like printing, chopsticks, and gunpowder. In several stories, the main character, always reacting the opposite of what is expected, is tricked by the smarter, minor characters.

HONOR

The Voyagers: Being Legends and Romances of Atlantic Discovery
Padraic Colum   Illustrated by Wildred Jones   Macmillan

Convinced that there is another land far away, Portugal's Prince Henry the Navigator gathers together all those who might know anything about it. In a high tower that overlooks the Atlantic Ocean, stories of legends and voyages are told along with those of the discoveries of Columbus and Ponce de León.

1925 AWARD

Tales from Silver Lands   Charles Finger
Illustrated by Charles Honore   Doubleday

Nineteen stories that Finger gathered from South American Indian villagers are retold retaining their original flavor. Included are captivating tales of witches, giants, and strange enchantments.

HONORS

Nicholas: A Manhattan Christmas Story   Annie Carroll Moore
Illustrated by Jay Van Everen   Putnam

Nicholas, eight inches high, is a little boy from Holland who visits New York City for a few months in the 1920s. While there, he attends parties, visits famous landmarks, and learns about the Dutch influence on the city. His first party is at the library, where he is introduced to many book characters.

The Dream Coach   Anne Parrish   Macmillan

The Dream Coach is pulled by one hundred misty horses. Helped by little angels, it travels the night sky dispensing dreams. Four children are introduced in turn, and their fairy-tale-like dreams, often involving inanimate objects that come to life, are shared.

1924 AWARD

The Dark Frigate   Charles Hawes
Illustrated by Anton Otto Fischer   Little, Brown

A seagoing adventure turns sour when the *Rose of Devon* is seized in mid-ocean by pirates. The vile, ruthless men force nineteen-year-old Philip to be a part of the pirate crew, and the hangman awaits his return to England. Set in the time of King Charles, the story does not romanticize piracy.

HONOR

No record.

1923 AWARD

The Voyages of Doctor Dolittle Hugh Lofting / Lippincott

Fun and nonsense reign as Dr. John Dolittle, a medical doctor and naturalist who has the ability to talk to animals, sets sail for Spider Monkey Island. There he unites two tribes, becomes king, and sails home inside the 70,000-year-old great glass sea snail. The story is told by the doctor's nine-and-a-half-year-old assistant.

HONOR

No record.

1922 AWARD

The Story of Mankind Hendrik Willem van Loon Liveright

Speaking directly to the reader, the author provides a fascinating picture of history from cave peoples to the present (1920). Ideas, movements, and people are more important than dates, and history is shown as something that builds upon itself.

HONORS

The Old Tobacco Shop: A True Account of What Befell a Little Boy in Search of Adventure William Bowen
Illustrated by Reginald Birch Macmillan

Fred is befriended by the hunchback who runs the tobacco shop. Warned never to smoke the magic tobacco in the porcelain jar shaped like a "Chinaman's head," Fred stays away from it for a long time. One day he falters and suddenly finds himself involved in high adventure on the Spanish Main.

The Golden Fleece and the Heroes Who Lived before Achilles Padraic Colum
Illustrated by Willy Pogany Macmillan

The ancient triumphs and tragedies of the Greek myths are woven through the central story of Jason and his quest for the Golden Fleece. The many stories told by Orpheus to the sailors in the story might be the very ones that the Argonauts heard on their long voyage.

The Great Quest   Charles Hawes   Illustrated by George Varian   Little, Brown

Twelve-year-old Josiah tells of how his Uncle Seth is tricked by an old friend into selling his shop and buying a ship. Thinking they are going in search of gold, Josiah and his uncle find themselves unwillingly involved in the slave trade and at odds with the crew.

Cedric the Forester   Bernard Marshall   Appleton

Cedric, son of a thirteenth-century forester, saves Sir Richard's son and is made his squire. Taught to read and fight, Cedric becomes the best crossbowman in England, and, at the Battle of the Eagles, he is knighted.

The Windy Hill   Cornelia Meigs   Macmillan

A brother and sister visit their older cousin in New England. Their cousin was once jovial but is now mysteriously irritable and preoccupied. A chance meeting with the beeman leads to their hearing stories about their own family's history. As they listen, the two children start to understand the cause of their cousin's anxiety.

The Caldecott Awards

2004—1938

2004 CALDECOTT AWARD

THE MAN WHO WALKED BETWEEN THE TOWERS

Mordicai Gerstein

Roaring Brook Press, a division of Millbrook

This true story recounts the daring feat of a spirited young Frenchman who walked a tightrope between the World Trade Center twin towers in 1974. His joy in dancing on a thin wire high above Manhattan and the awe of the spectators in the streets far below are captured in exquisite ink and oil paintings that perfectly complement the spare, lyrical text.

"Gerstein's skillful compositions and dramatic use of perspective make this a book that literally takes your breath away," said Caldecott Award Chair Kathy East. "Two ingenious gatefolds and horizontal and vertical framing put the reader high in the air with this daredevil performer and emphasize the vast space between the towers and their astounding height. Gerstein ensures that this extraordinary event is imprinted on readers' minds and creates a powerful, transforming memory."

MORDICAI GERSTEIN

2004 HONOR BOOKS

Ella Sarah Gets Dressed   Margaret Chodos-Irvine   Harcourt

Standing in front of her wardrobe, Ella Sarah selects her attire. "I want to wear my pink polka-dot pants, my dress with orange-and-green flowers, my purple-and-blue striped socks, my yellow shoes, and my red hat." Her parents and siblings try to persuade her to wear something more conservative. Ella Sarah emphatically responds, "No!" and makes her own fashion statement.

Elegant in its simplicity, *Ella Sarah Gets Dressed* is a classic picture book that uses a "variety of printmaking techniques." Cheerful, bold colors outlined in white emphasize Ella Sarah's freedom and confidence. Pink polka-dots on an orange background and blue-green rickrack on the borders of the jacket flap foreshadow her unique outfit. With careful attention to detail and design, the imaginative use of colors and illustrations that convey emotions make this a fun visual experience.

What Do You Do with a Tail like This?   Steve Jenkins and Robin Page   Houghton

This innovative guessing book delivers a fun and playful science lesson on thirty animals' body parts: ears, eyes, mouths, noses, feet, and tails. The artist uses exquisite cut-paper collage to detail basic forms combined with clever placement of the spare text to create an interactive visual display.

A masterly blend of textured paper, image, and white space, and the clever use of the book's elements create tension and humor.

Don't Let the Pigeon Drive the Bus   Mo Willems   Hyperion

A persistent pigeon asks, pleads, cajoles, wheedles, connives, negotiates, demands, and uses emotional blackmail in attempts to get behind the wheel. Pigeon will not take no for an answer and puts the reader on the spot, using an escalating series of tactics. Even a temper tantrum is futile, but not the end of Pigeon's dreams.

Willems portrays the wide-ranging emotions and the personality of this pigeon with just a few deft strokes of a crayon and a limited palette of colors. Perfectly paced, every line and blank space in the deceptively simple illustrations are essential to this distinguished work.

2003 AWARD

My Friend Rabbit   Eric Rohmann   Millbrook

Mouse shares his brand-new toy airplane with his friend Rabbit, and no one can predict the disastrous—but hilarious—results. When the airplane lands in a tree, the chaos only builds as Rabbit drags, pushes, and carries the whole neighborhood, including Elephant, Hippo, and Crocodile, to aid in the rescue. Eric Rohmann's hand-colored relief prints express a vibrant energy through solid black outlines, lightly textured backgrounds, and a robust use of color.

HONORS

The Spider and the Fly   Mary Howitt
Illustrated by Tony DiTerlizzi   Simon & Schuster

DiTerlizzi's wickedly delicious tribute to silent film—based on the cautionary tale penned by Mary Howitt in 1829—presents an old-fashioned cackling villain and a naive damsel in distress in this ambient, moody picture book with all the allure of the flickering silver screen. Skillful use of tone, line, and perspective add to the mystery of this melodramatic tale, executed entirely in eerie shades of black and white.

Hondo & Fabian   Peter McCarty   Holt

A beach outing for the dog and a full day at home for the cat are skillfully interwoven in this quiet tale of friendship. Spare text describes the day's events while soft, glowing illustrations tell the real story of parallel activities with subtle humor. McCarty's design choices from font and page layout to size and inviting cover art show great attention to detail in this masterfully executed picture book.

Noah's Ark   Jerry Pinkney   North-South

In this striking rendition of Noah and the Great Flood, Jerry Pinkney has integrated the well-known story from Genesis with masterful pencil and watercolor illustrations to create a stunning whole. Vibrant paintings evoke the tone of the story from lush, sweeping views of the earth to intricate details of the massive ark, myriad animals, Noah and his family, and finally to the restoration of the planet.

2002 AWARD

The Three Pigs   David Wiesner   Houghton/Clarion

In *The Three Pigs,* the plot and form of a familiar folktale unravel as the pigs are huffed and puffed off the page andto a new world. The trio cavorts through scenes from a nursery rhyme to a fairy tale, liberating other characters on the fly. Using a range of artistic styles and thrilling perspectives, Wiesner plays with the structure and conventions of traditional storytelling, redefining the picture book.

HONORS

Martin's Big Words: The Life of Dr. Martin Luther King, Jr.
Doreen Rappaport   Illustrated by Bryan Collier
Hyperion Books for Children/Jump at the Sun

> In this picture-book biography of Martin Luther King Jr., Rappaport's spare text and carefully chosen quotes are carried to a powerful emotional level by Collier's art. From the smiling, inviting image on the cover to each striking double spread the artist portrays significant events evoking King's purpose, telling readers that "his big words are alive for us today."

The Dinosaurs of Waterhouse Hawkins: An Illuminating History of Mr. Waterhouse Hawkins, Artist and Lecturer   Barbara Kerley
Illustrated by Brian Selznick   Scholastic

> With a sense of showmanship echoing the spectacle of Waterhouse Hawkins's own public presentations, this dramatic biography brings the work of the nineteenth-century dinosaur artist to life. Using a rich palette, theatrical staging, and monumental dimensions, Selznick creates an exquisite balance between illustration and design in this distinguished marriage of science and art.

The Stray Dog   Marc Simont   HarperCollins

> A chance encounter turns into a family love affair in this disarmingly simple, gently humorous, and emotionally satisfying tale. The soft palette and subtle touches in the distinctive watercolors perfectly capture the heroic actions of the young protagonists and convey the universal feelings of longing and belonging.

2001 AWARD

So You Want to Be President   Judith St. George
Illustrated by David Small   Philomel/Penguin Putnam

In illustrations rendered in a harmonious mix of watercolor, ink, and pastel chalk, Small employs wiry and expansive lines that echo political cartooning and invest this personable history of the presidency with imaginative detail, wry humor, and refreshing dignity. Small's illustrations capture the spirit of each president featured and provide a genuinely enlightening overview of this unique American institution.

HONORS

Casey at the Bat: A Ballad of the Republic Sung in the Year 1888
Ernest Lawrence Thayer   Illustrated by Christopher Bing   Handprint

> In the format of an 1888 scrapbook, the immortal ballad of Ernest Thayer finds new life in Christopher Bing's innovative treatment. Pen-and-ink scratchboard

"engravings" in late nineteenth-century style seamlessly blend memorabilia and trompe l'oeil re-creations in an homage to the great American pastime.

Click, Clack, Moo: Cows That Type   Doreen Cronin
Illustrated by Betsy Lewin   Simon & Schuster

Farm-smart cows recycle a piece of outdated technology, a manual typewriter, to improve barnyard conditions. Lewin's illustrations help tell this tongue-in-cheek story about bovine agitators locking horns with Farmer Brown in a battle of will and wit that results in a comically satisfying conclusion.

Olivia   Ian Falconer   Simon & Schuster

Olivia, an inquisitive, creative, confident young piglet, is "very good at wearing people out." With the touch of a minimalist, Falconer has created an exuberant character using deft black lines, delicate charcoal shading, generous white space, and spots of brilliant red.

2000 AWARD

Joseph Had a Little Overcoat   Simms Taback   Viking

A resourceful and resilient tailor transforms his wornout overcoat into smaller and smaller garments. The book is illustrated in watercolor, gouache, pencil, ink, and collage. The patchwork layout of the pages, the two-dimensional paintings, and the exaggerated perspectives, reminiscent of the folk art tradition, are the very fabric that turn this overcoat into a story.

HONORS

A Child's Calendar   John Updike
Illustrated by Trina Schart Hyman   Holiday House

Twelve seasonal poems spanning the calendar year are accompanied by pen and ink and watercolor paintings that complement and enhance the text in this book of poetry. Hyman's affectionate illustrations expand Updike's poetic celebration of the changing of the seasons and holidays.

Sector 7   David Wiesner   Clarion

A small boy on a class trip to the Empire State Building is transported by a friendly cloud to Sector 7, a great cloud factory high in the sky. Wiesner's striking and dramatic watercolors transform the childhood fantasy of figures in the clouds into an imaginative story without words.

When Sophie Gets Angry—Really, Really Angry
Molly Bang   Scholastic

> Sophie's indignation over being required to share a favorite toy with her sister leads her on a lonely internal journey from anger to equilibrium. Bang's use of color, line, and visual onomatopoeia combine with a deceptively simple text to create a visually stunning color of a child's journey through a temper tantrum and back to the warmth of her family.

The Ugly Duckling   Adapted and illustrated
by Jerry Pinkney   Morrow

> Panoramic end papers set the scene for the creation of the familiar Hans Christian Andersen tale, *The Ugly Duckling*. Each full-page spread is lush with color that befits the beauty of the naturalistic setting. Pinkney imbues the animals with personality without anthropomorphizing them.

1999 AWARD

Snowflake Bentley   Jacqueline Briggs Martin
Illustrated by Mary Azarian   Houghton

Mary Azarian's handsome woodcuts recall the impassioned life of a self-taught Vermont scientist, who as a boy was determined that one day his camera would capture the extraordinary and unique beauty of snowflakes.

HONORS

Duke Ellington: The Piano Prince and His Orchestra   Andrea Davis Pinkney
Illustrated by Brian Pinkney   Hyperion

> Brian Pinkney masterfully uses color and movement to introduce today's children to the life and music of Duke Ellington, one of the great composers and jazz musicians of the twentieth century.

No, David!   David Shannon   Blue Sky/Scholastic

> David, a typically mischievous preschooler, is into everything he shouldn't be and "No, David!" is his mother's constant refrain. Shannon's childlike paintings and inventive use of line, color, and perspective bring David to life.

Snow   Uri Shulevitz   Farrar Straus Giroux

> This magical picture book captures in ink and watercolor washes the excitement of a small boy and his dog who, despite adult naysayers, steadfastly believe that snow is coming.

Tibet: Through the Red Box   Peter Sís
Frances Foster Books/Farrar Straus Giroux

> Through detailed art and lyrical text, Sís takes the reader on a literal, spiritual, and symbolic journey through time and memory to his childhood, his separation from a father far away in Tibet, and finally their reunion.

1998 AWARD

Rapunzel   Paul O. Zelinsky   Dutton

Zelinsky retells the story based on the familiar Grimm's folktale as well as earlier French and Italian sources. The detailed oil paintings are inspired by Renaissance Masters' paintings.

HONORS

The Gardener   Sarah Stewart   Illustrated by David Small   Farrar

> Illustrations, combined with letters home, tell the story of Lydia Grace Finch, a young Depression-era heroine, who transforms her curmudgeonly uncle and his dreary urban neighborhood with her rooftop garden.

Harlem   Walter Dean Myers   Illustrated by Christopher Myers   Scholastic

> Christopher Myers uses ink, gouache, and cut-paper collage to interpret his father's ode to Harlem. A kaleidoscope of words and images leads the reader on a musical journey filled with sass and swing.

There Was an Old Lady Who Swallowed a Fly   Simms Taback   Viking

> The popular American folk song of the old woman with an insatiable taste for life is served up in a fresh presentation. The reader is treated to an insider's view of her progressively excessive appetite through expanding die-cut peepholes to the inevitable climax.

1997 AWARD

Golem   David Wisniewski   Clarion

The Jews in sixteenth-century Prague turn to their rabbi during time of trouble. The Golem, created to protect the Jews, reflects the themes of power and redemption. How the rabbi deals with the soulless clay giant is a tale that is detailed through intricate paper-cuts.

HONORS

Hush! A Thai Lullaby   Minfong Ho
Illustrated by Holly Meade   Melanie Kroupa/Orchard

> A strong visual narrative tells the story of a mother who warns a crying mosquito, a leaping frog, and a swinging monkey not to waken her sleeping child. This is a gentle, cumulative bedtime story, sure to please and settle down children.

The Graphic Alphabet   David Pelletier   Edited by Neal Porter   Orchard

> This alphabet book uses computer imagery laced with wit and humor to help young children learn the letters. Each letter is not only represented by a word, image, or concept but also is the word, image, or concept. Crisp imagery is combined with meticulous design.

The Paperboy   Dav Pilkey   Jackson/Orchard

> A boy wakes in the darkness, bundles his newspapers, and accompanied by his faithful dog delivers the daily papers to the still, dark houses. Carefully balanced compositions and a restrained but rich palette give this story tremendous visual appeal.

Starry Messenger   Peter Sís   Frances Foster Books/Farrar Straus Giroux

> Galileo Galilei's story is illustrated in a style that evokes Renaissance art, architecture, and cartography. The events of his everyday life, the struggles and successes, are captured through detailed attention on each page, which brings to life the world on the verge of discovery.

1996 AWARD

Officer Buckle and Gloria   Peggy Rathmann   Putnam

Police dog Gloria's irreverent acrobatics behind Safety Officer Buckle's back contrast with the officer's straight-laced safety tips to school audiences. Original, lively, and energetic art leads the readers through a story of cooperation and friendship. Watercolor and ink illustrations employ brilliant colors that, combined with a creative use of white space, engage the reader in the humor and warmth of this stellar performance.

HONORS

Alphabet City   Stephen T. Johnson   Viking

> Photorealistic paintings of urban environment present an imaginative variety of views and perspectives, textures, and light. Each painting stands alone as a handsome, balanced piece. Together they are an inspiring exercise in seeing patterns and art in everyday things.

Zin! Zin! Zin! a Violin Lloyd Moss
Illustrated by Marjorie Priceman Simon & Schuster

> This exuberant introduction to the orchestra is a true celebration of music. The sense of visual musicality is enhanced by warm, changing background colors. The musicians themselves are far from static, and the text has rhythm and punch, changing size and moving across the pages in swoops and swirls to reflect the flow of music.

The Faithful Friend Robert D. San Souci
Illustrated by Brian Pinkney Simon & Schuster

> Pinkney's distinctive illustrations evoke the mystery, magic, and romance in San Souci's retelling of this West Indian folktale. The unique scratchboard style, enhanced by vivid oil colors, is a superb match for this atmospheric story in which the main characters confront and ultimately overcome the dark forces of evil.

Tops & Bottoms Adapted and illustrated by Janet Stevens Harcourt

> Sleepy, sprawling bear is outwitted by the wily hare, who succeeds in feeding his numerous offspring with abundant vegetable harvests. Handmade vegetable paper and a masterful use of mixed media contribute to this zesty, organic combination of story and illustration.

1995 AWARD

Smoky Night Eve Bunting Illustrated by David Diaz Harcourt

Inspired by the Los Angeles riots, *Smoky Night* relates the happenings of a night of urban rioting from a child's perspective. With thickly textured, expressionistic acrylic paintings set against mixed-media collages, Diaz creates dramatic, groundbreaking illustrations of the night's events. Both language and illustration convey the universal importance of human interaction through the personal story of one little boy and his cat.

HONORS

Swamp Angel Anne Isaacs Illustrated by Paul O. Zelinsky Dutton

> In this original tall tale, Angelica Longrider, known as Swamp Angel, wrestles the huge bear Thundering Tarnation to save the winter supplies of settlers in Tennessee. With his whimsical illustrations, Paul O. Zelinsky has created a memorable heroine with the grit and gusto of a Paul Bunyan. Primitive-style oil paint-

ings on cherry, maple, and birch veneers capture the folksy feel of life in nine-teenth-century Tennessee.

John Henry   Julius Lester   Illustrated by Jerry Pinkney   Dial

Pinkney's earthy, craggy pencil and watercolor illustrations capture both the power and the humanity of this African-American folk-hero. Masterful use of light and shadow portray the strength and mass of the Allegheny mountains, which match the magnitude of John Henry, while delicate shading and mottled color suggest the detail of a realistic natural setting enlivened with touches of whimsy.

Time Flies   Eric Rohmann   Crown

Stunning oil paintings in this wordless picture book dramatically portray a bird's flight though a museum display into the age of the living dinosaurs, where it encounters creatures vastly larger than itself. Rohmann uses rich, realistic shading; texture; and varying perspectives to create the bird's fanciful journey back to the time of its primitive ancestors.

1994 AWARD

Grandfather's Journey   Allen Say   Edited by Walter Lorraine   Houghton

Grandfather's Journey eloquently portrays a Japanese immigrant's travels to a new land. Exquisite watercolors portray vast landscapes along with intimate family portraits that communicate hope, dignity, sadness, and love. Say powerfully connects the personal and the universal to create a rare harmony of longing and belonging.

HONORS

Peppe the Lamplighter   Elisa Bartone
Illustrated by Ted Lewin   Lothrop

Lewin vividly captures the bustling market scenes, bleak tenement rooms, and the lamplit streets of turn-of-the-century New York's Little Italy. Dramatic watercolors portray young Peppe's struggle to help support his immigrant family and to win his father's respect.

In the Small, Small Pond   Denise Fleming   Holt

Bright colors and lively language describe the cycle of pond life. Rhyming alliterative text and vibrant illustrations are filled with movement and fun in a joyous celebration of the natural world. Fleming created the illustration by pouring colored pulp through hand-cut stencils.

Owen   Kevin Henkes   Greenwillow

A preschooler mouse, Owen, and his concerned parents confront a classic childhood drama: releasing the trusty, fuzzy blanket. Confident economical line and inspired layout convey Owen's spirited tenacity as he dances toward greater independence.

Raven: A Trickster Tale from the Pacific Northwest
Gerald McDermott   Harcourt

McDermott reshapes the familiar trickster tale from the Pacific Northwest in which Raven steals light from the Sky Chief and brings it to people. Raven's spirit world is boldly colored and hard-edged, a strong graphic contrast to the soft watercolor background of the real Northwest landscape.

Yo! Yes?   Chris Raschka   Edited by Richard Jackson   Orchard

Through bold, original use of line and angle, color and space, Raschka celebrates friendship and offers a timeless message about taking risks.The brief, rhythmic text invites enthusiastic sharing.

1993 AWARD

Mirette on the High Wire   Emily Arnold McCully   Putnam

Emily Arnold McCully's vivid impressionistic watercolors bring nineteenth-century Paris to life with the story of Mirette, a spirited, risk-taking little girl. Mirette enables the former high-wire star Bellini to conquer his fear while achieving her own dream. Light, color, line, and movement in these animated and bold illustrations are in perfect balance with the text.

HONORS

The Stinky Cheese Man & Other Fairly Stupid Tales   Jon Scieszka
Illustrated by Lane Smith   Viking

The Little Red Hen talks in red letters and the giant talks in capitals in this irreverent retelling of the gingerbread man and other time-honored tales. The avant-garde art ("rendered in oil and vinegar" according to the book note) lampoons twentieth-century art in the process. Interdependence of words, visual images, and even the process of book design and publication extract every possible laugh in this outrageous collaboration.

Working Cotton   Sherley Anne Williams
Illustrated by Carole Byard   Harcourt

> Carole Byard's dramatic paintings portray the dignity of hard work and the strength of family relationships that are part of this migrant family's life. From the first glimpses of a streaky dawn to the red twilight, powerful, glowing portraits and landscapes poignantly complement the child's poetic depiction of the long work-day.

Seven Blind Mice   Ed Young   Philomel

> In this successful reinterpretation of the Indian fable of the blind man and the elephant, deceptively simple text integrates concepts of color, numbers, and days of the week with visual irony. Contrasting textured paper heightens the bold color and strong composition, while white typeface against a glossy background and marbleized endpapers add to the excellent design.

1992 AWARD

Tuesday   David Wiesner   Clarion

Flying frogs on lily pads create mischief as they move from the fen to a small town on a Tuesday evening. The story ends with a comic twist suggesting more fantastic flights for the following Tuesday. Wiesner's watercolor illustrations show masterful use of light and dark, alternating perspectives, and variation in page design in this nine-word book.

HONOR

Tar Beach   Faith Ringgold   Crown

> Child Cassie flies high above New York City in the 1930s, high above the quilt squares that ground each page, high above the busyness and conflict of everyday life, from family rooftop picnics to daddy's construction work. Acrylic paintings on canvas paper form the basis of this visual feast celebrating the act of transformation, while the quilt form represents an historically important African-American communication medium.

1991 AWARD

Black and White   David Macaulay   Houghton

Macaulay interweaves fantasy and reality in a tale of parents, trains, and cows. The author recommends careful inspection of words and pictures to both minimize and enhance confusion.

HONORS

Puss in Boots   Fred Marcellino   di Capua/Farrar

Large pale type and golden-toned paintings work brilliantly together providing an elegant regal look to the familiar fairy tale of Puss. With varied perspectives and points of view, Marcellino re-creates the French court and countryside to ingenious, often droll, effect.

"More, More, More," Said the Baby: 3 Love Stories
Vera B. Williams   Greenwillow

Brightly framed gouache paintings reflect each child's sense of security and joy as a loving adult "catches" that baby up. This creative use of color, shape, and rhythm marks a unique and distinctive celebration of family life.

1990 AWARD

Lon Po Po: A Red-Riding Hood Story from China
Ed Young   Philomel

Suspense and drama are lightened with bits of humor as the wolf Lon Po Po tries to trick three children into letting him into their house. Though he succeeds, the children quickly turn the tables on the wily animal. The artist uses vivid watercolors and pastels to create dramatic panel pictures.

HONORS

Color Zoo   Lois Ehlert   Lippincott

Vibrant colors and overlays of geometric-shaped cutouts in heavy paper combine to create expressive animal faces. The text is simply a one-word identification of the shape or animal. All of the action is in the creative paper engineering.

Hershel and the Hanukkah Goblins   Eric Kimmel
Illustrated by Trina Schart Hyman   Holiday House

Eight goblins haunt the old synagogue, preventing the villagers from celebrating Hanukkah until Hershel arrives to outwit all of the creatures. The dark illustrations are charged with energy as they show the imaginatively wicked goblins trying to frighten Hershel away.

Bill Peet: An Autobiography   Bill Peet   Houghton

From the time he learned to manipulate a crayon, drawing has been a consuming passion for Bill Peet. He tells how that passion affected his life, from childhood, through his work at the Disney Studios, to his life as an author. Using his usual artistic style, Peet has filled his autobiography with new black-and-white illustrations.

The Talking Eggs   Robert D. San Souci   Illustrated by Jerry Pinkney   Dial

Running away from her angry mother and spoiled sister, Blanche is befriended by a strange old woman who owns a cow with two heads and chickens that lay talking eggs. The eerie and suspenseful black folktale is filled with watercolor pictures of deep woods and strange sights.

1989 AWARD

Song and Dance Man   Karen Ackerman
Illustrated by Stephen Gammell   Knopf

When his grandchildren come to visit, Grandpa whisks them up to the attic, where he performs an exciting vaudeville routine. The colored-pencil sketches are alive with movement and drama.

HONORS

Mirandy and Brother Wind   Patricia C. McKissack
Illustrated by Jerry Pinkney   Knopf

A sparkling, energetic Mirandy vows to dance with the wind at her first cakewalk—but to do that, she must catch it first. Lush, expansive illustrations of the rural South capture the vigor and imagination of the story.

Goldilocks and the Three Bears   Illustrated by James Marshall   Dial

The antithesis of the typical sweet, demure Goldilocks, this little girl with her bouncing golden ringlets is brash, irreverent, and captivating. Set in the present day, the briefly told nursery story abounds with color, humor, and wit.

The Boy of the Three-Year Nap   Diane Snyder
Illustrated by Allen Say   Houghton

Taro has earned his nickname because of his laziness and penchant for sleeping. When he turns trickster to stop his industrious mother's nagging, she in turn outwits him. The handsome pictures are noticeably influenced by eighteenth-century Japanese woodcuts and reflect the culture of the land where this folktale originated.

Free Fall   Illustrated by David Wiesner   Lothrop

In a book made more powerful because it has no words to stifle the imagination, a boy falls asleep and dreams of fantastic adventures. In this visual story, the objects around the boy evolve from one thing into another and then back to their original shapes.

1988 AWARD

Owl Moon   Jane Yolen   Illustrated by John Schoenherr   Philomel

Late one quiet winter's night, a little girl and her father go owling, watching and listening for the signs that say a great horned owl is nearby. Blue-toned color washes and simple landscapes create a frosty, magical night perfect for owl watching.

HONOR

Mufaro's Beautiful Daughters: An African Tale   John Steptoe   Lothrop

Of the two sisters, one kind and good, the other mean and deceitful, only one will be chosen to marry the king. Dramatic yet realistic paintings in lush, jewel-toned colors illustrate this folktale from Zimbabwe.

1987 AWARD

Hey, Al   Arthur Yorinks   Illustrated by Richard Egielski   Farrar

Janitor Al and his dog are swept away from their apparently humdrum lives by a huge bird that takes them to what at first seems like paradise. Full-color illustrations provide florid scenes of that paradise.

HONORS

The Village of Round and Square Houses   Ann Grifalconi   Little, Brown

Pastel drawings are used to illustrate the story of the remote Cameron village of Tos where the women live in the round houses and the men live in the square ones so that each has a place to be together and a place to be apart.

Alphabatics   Suse MacDonald   Bradbury

Brightly colored letters of the alphabet become acrobats as they twist and turn until they become the objects that represent the letters: A becomes an ark, J becomes a jack-in-the-box, S becomes a swan.

Rumpelstiltskin   Paul O. Zelinsky   Dutton

When the proud father tells the king that his daughter can spin straw into gold, it is the tiny Rumpelstiltskin who actually does the spinning—for the price of the first-born child. Golden-toned, full-color oil paintings in medieval style retell this tale based on an early Brothers Grimm version.

1986 AWARD

The Polar Express   Chris Van Allsburg   Houghton

Dark, brooding illustrations with unusual perspectives set the mood for a magical and poignant train ride. It is Christmas Eve when the young boy boards the train for a trip to the North Pole. There he receives a special gift from Santa Claus.

HONORS

The Relatives Came   Cynthia Rylant
Illustrated by Stephen Gammell   Bradbury

> What a marvelous time is had when all the relatives come from Virginia for a visit! They crowd into the house, where there is much loving and hugging and breathing to do together! The pictures nearly bounce off the pages with all the love and happiness in this book.

King Bidgood's in the Bathtub   Audrey Wood
Illustrated by Don Wood   Harcourt

> When the court is in a dither because the king refuses to get out of the bathtub, only the young page knows what to do. Illustrations reminiscent of an opera stage setting show off the full glory of the court scenes.

1985 AWARD

Saint George and the Dragon   Retold by Margaret Hodges
Illustrated by Trina Schart Hyman   Little, Brown

Lady Una and George, a knight of the Red Cross, must find and battle the terrible dragon that ruins the land. Hyman's illustrations tell the story dramatically, and the reader seems to look at the scenes through an iron-encased window.

HONORS

Hansel and Gretel   Retold by Rika Lesser
Illustrated by Paul O. Zelinsky   Dodd

> In this book translated from one of the less-embellished versions of the classic Brothers Grimm story, the artwork dominates. Sometimes imitating sixteenth- and seventeenth-century Flemish art, sometimes adopting a romantic nineteenth-century style, the paintings are rich in color and detail.

The Story of Jumping Mouse   Retold and illustrated by John Steptoe   Lothrop

> Large, expressive pencil drawings help tell the tale of a field mouse's search for the Far-Off Land. Armed with courage and hope, the mouse overcomes many obsta-

cles until it is transformed into an eagle. The text is freely adapted from an unidentified Native American "why" story.

Have You Seen My Duckling?   Nancy Tafuri   Greenwillow

In this almost wordless book, a duck asks the creatures of the pond if they have seen her lost duckling. Bright, clear illustrations show the adventuresome duckling, who is always seen a little hidden from but close to his mother.

1984 AWARD

The Glorious Flight: Across the Channel with Louis Blériot
Alice and Martin Provensen   Viking

Once he sees a flying machine, Louis Blériot becomes passionately interested in building his own machine and is successful on his eleventh attempt. Based on a true incident in France in the early 1900s, the biography is illustrated with pictures of shifting perspectives and touches of humor and views of a family growing older.

HONORS

Ten, Nine, Eight   Molly Bang   Greenwillow

Bedtime becomes a favorite time as the countdown begins. In a lulling rhyme, all of the things in a little girl's room are counted. The quiet time shared between father and daughter is illustrated with warm colors.

Little Red Riding Hood   Retold and illustrated by Trina Schart Hyman   Holiday

The familiar story of the little girl who goes to visit her grandmother subtly warns children not to talk to strangers. The detailed illustrations seem to place the setting of the story in New England.

1983 AWARD

Shadow   Blaise Cendrars
Translated and illustrated by Marcia Brown   Scribner

Translated from the French poet Blaise Cendrars' work, this symbolic mood piece reflects stories told by African storytellers and shamans around a nighttime fire. Rich colors with black cutout accents create the visual image of the prowling, dancing, mute shadow.

HONORS

When I Was Young in the Mountains   Cynthia Rylant
Illustrated by Diane Goode   Dutton

> The author affectionately recalls a childhood spent with her family in the Appalachian Mountains of West Virginia. Warm family scenes are filled with friendly, happy people. Many of the illustrations drift off into the mountain mist and bring a peacefulness to the recalled pleasures.

A Chair for My Mother   Vera B. Williams   Greenwillow

> After a fire destroys their home, a little girl, her waitress mother, and the girl's grandmother move into an apartment. They start saving all their coins for a big, comfortable chair for Mama and Grandma. The watercolor paintings have a suitably childlike look.

1982 AWARD

Jumanji   Chris Van Allsburg   Houghton

Looking for something to do on a boring afternoon, Peter and Judy decide to try the strange board game they find in the park. Boredom vanishes as every space on which they land comes to life. Meticulously crafted black-and-white illustrations bring the game alive.

HONORS

Where the Buffaloes Begin   Olaf Baker
Illustrated by Stephen Gammell   Warne

> Majestic, haunting, and moody gray-toned illustrations show Little Wolf on his journey to the sacred place where buffaloes are said to originate. The rich prose was first published in *St. Nicholas Magazine* in 1915.

On Market Street   Arnold Lobel   Illustrated by Anita Lobel   Greenwillow

> A nursery rhyme-like verse breaks into a celebration of all the wares—from A to Z—that a little boy purchases on Market Street. The illustrations, based on seventeenth-century French trade engravings, show brightly colored shopkeepers composed of their merchandise.

Outside over There   Maurice Sendak   Harper

> When Ida is not focusing her complete attention on her baby sister, the baby is kidnapped by hooded goblins and replaced by a baby made of ice. Elaborate paintings combine romantic and surrealistic effects and are filled with subtleties and symbolism.

A Visit to William Blake's Inn: Poems for Innocent and Experienced Travelers
Nancy Willard   Illustrated by Alice and Martin Provensen   Harcourt

Lyrical poems written in the spirit of William Blake combine with captivatingly imaginative illustrations that reflect the staidness and the whimsy of the eighteenth century. Nancy Willard also won the 1982 Newbery Award for this book.

1981 AWARD

Fables   Arnold Lobel   Harper

Twenty original, brief, and witty animal fables, each complete with a moral, expose human foibles. Each fable is faced with a full-page painting in soft, rich colors that show the droll animals at the crucial moment of the fable.

HONORS

The Grey Lady and the Strawberry Snatcher   Molly Bang   Four Winds

An old lady who, except for her hands and face, appears as a grey silhouette, buys a basket of strawberries and proceeds home, pursued by a strawberry snatcher. Interesting colors and textures are effectively combined with negative grey shapes in this vivid visual hide-and-seek game.

Truck   Donald Crews   Greenwillow

Bright colors and geometric shapes roll across the pages as a truck carries a cargo of tricycles to its destination. There is no text. From the loading dock, through intricate highway systems, past road signs, to a truck stop, in clear and stormy weather, the big red truck moves its precious cargo across the country.

Mice Twice   Joseph Low   McElderry/Atheneum

Cat is very hungry and wants a nice tender mouse to eat, so he invites Mouse to dinner. Things escalate until even Lion and Crocodile are involved. It is Wasp who settles things in this funny tale that is enhanced through whimsical drawings.

The Bremen-Town Musicians   Retold and illustrated by Ilse Plume   Doubleday

Four animals, all unwanted, set out together to become musicians but instead end up outwitting a band of robbers. The Brothers Grimm tale is illustrated with glowing, subdued colors and rounded shapes.

1980 AWARD

Ox-Cart Man   Donald Hall   Illustrated by Barbara Cooney   Viking

Clean, uncluttered paintings capture the flavor of nineteenth-century New England as a family's day-to-day life is mandated by the changing season. There is a strong sense of the passage of time and rhythm of life in this book.

HONORS

Ben's Trumpet   Rachel Isadora   Greenwillow

The mood, sounds, and rhythms of jazz pulsate through the illustrations as Ben sits on the fire escape and blows his imaginary trumpet to the jazz sounds eminating from the Zig Zig Jazz Club. Set in the twenties and illustrated with dynamic black-and-white drawings, this is the story of one boy's dream coming true.

The Treasure   Uri Shulevitz   Farrar

A poor man dreams that he must go to the castle bridge and wait for something that will turn about his fortunes. Traveling far to get there, he learns that the treasure is under his own stove. Illustrations with softly glowing colors and a striking use of light depict traditional eastern European villages and countrysides.

The Garden of Abdul Gasazi   Chris Van Allsburg   Houghton

Illusion and reality become blurred when the unruly dog the boy has been tending runs away into the secret, foreboding garden of a retired magician. The visual perspectives and the play of light on the gray pencil drawings create an eerie, mysterious feeling.

1979 AWARD

The Girl Who Loved Wild Horses   Paul Goble   Bradbury

The kinship is so strong between a Plains Indian girl and the horses she has lived with since becoming lost in a storm, that eventually she becomes one of them. Sharp, brilliantly colored paintings sweep across the pages and are in perfect harmony with the story.

HONORS

Freight Train   Donald Crews   Greenwillow

Large pictures of the different freight cars are identified by name and by color. Soon the train begins to move into a blur of colors as it swiftly goes on its way.

The Way to Start a Day   Byrd Baylor   Illustrated by Peter Parnall   Scribner

A vibrant sunflower yellow and other colors blend with crisp, black lines to make effective use of symbolism in celebration of the sun. Poetic prose tells how cultures throughout the ages have sung to the new day's sun to honor it.

1978 AWARD

Noah's Ark   Peter Spier   Doubleday

The only text is the seventeenth-century Dutch poem, "The Flood," by Jacobus Revius, that opens the book. The rest of the book is a visual interpretation of Noah and his unbelievably difficult task of tending the animals on the ark. Careful details and softly hued watercolors depict the story with reverence, humor, and delight.

HONORS

Castle   David Macaulay   Houghton

Macaulay traces in text and drawings the step-by-step construction of a fictitious thirteenth-century English castle in Wales from its conception to its baptism by fire—a direct attack by hundreds of Welsh soldiers. The complex engineering task is generously illustrated with detailed black-and-white line drawings and diagrams.

It Could Always Be Worse   Retold and illustrated by Margot Zemach   Farrar

Crowded into one room with his mother, wife, and six children, a man goes to the rabbi for help. The rabbi's answer is to bring one animal after another to live in the house. Dynamic, earth-toned paintings with an eastern European look capture the humor of the rabbi's good advice.

1977 AWARD

Ashanti to Zulu: African Traditions   Margaret Musgrove
Illustrated by Leo and Diane Dillon   Dial

Twenty-six different African tribal traditions and customs are introduced using the English alphabet as the vehicle. A border on each page frames the text and illustrations, where glowing colors mix with rich browns. The attention to authentic detail in each painting is remarkable.

HONORS

Hawk, I'm Your Brother   Byrd Baylor   Illustrated by Peter Parnall   Scribner

In a gentle story told in simple, poetic prose, a young Native American boy wants desperately to fly like a hawk. Spacious, clean, panoramic line drawings convey the yearning of the boy and the power of the hawk.

Fish for Supper   M. B. Goffstein   Dial

This quiet story chronicles the simple daily routine of Grandma, whose life centers around fishing. The black-and-white line drawings are centered in a square border of white space.

The Contest   Retold and illustrated by Nonny Hogrogian   Greenwillow

Realizing that they are both engaged to the same woman and each unwilling to give her up, two robbers compare their cleverness in thievery to see who deserves her. Large, colorful illustrations capture the flavor of the Armenian culture in this humorous folktale.

The Golem   Beverly Brodsky McDermott   Lippincott

The somber Jewish legend of the Golem, a creature created from clay that becomes more powerful and terrible than the evil he was made to destroy, is re-created with high visual drama. Striking paintings, vibrant with deep, rich colors, are filled with symbolism and massive shapes.

The Amazing Bone   William Steig   Farrar

On her way home from school, hapless heroine Pearl Pig finds an amazing talking bone. When the delectable piglet is waylaid by a debonair fox, the amazing bone saves Pearl. Sunny, fresh, springtime landscapes provide the background for the well-dressed characters.

1976 AWARD

Why Mosquitoes Buzz in People's Ears   Retold by Verna Aardema
Illustrated by Leo and Diane Dillon   Dial

Mosquito tells Iguana a tall tale about yams that annoys Iguana so much that he puts sticks in his ears so he cannot hear such things. Thus begins a chain reaction tale of the West African jungle. Illustrations show highly stylized animals.

HONORS

The Desert Is Theirs   Byrd Baylor   Illustrated by Peter Parnall   Scribner

A spare, lyrical text tells of the relationship of the Papagos people to their environment—"we share . . . we only share." The paintings are dramatic and are reminiscent of the layers of colors found in sand paintings.

Strega Nona   Tomie de Paola   Prentice-Hall

Strega Nona leaves Big Anthony alone with her magic pasta pot after telling him never to touch it. It is not long before he does, and pasta literally flows through the town. Characters in medieval costumes of pastel, jewel-like colors add to the humor of the story.

1975 AWARD

Arrow to the Sun   Gerald McDermott   Viking

The son of the Lord of the Sun sets out to find his father in this adaptation of a Pueblo legend. On his way, he undergoes four trials to prove his relationship to the Sun. The stylized, strong geometric art vividly portrays the desert and its intense sun colors.

HONOR

Jambo Means Hello   Muriel Feelings   Illustrated by Tom Feelings   Dial

Letters of the alphabet are represented by words of the Swahili language. A brief explanation of the word includes cultural information of East African countries. Beautiful full-page illustrations further depict the cultures.

1974 AWARD

Duffy and the Devil   Retold by Harve Zemach
Illustrated by Margot Zemach   Farrar

The Cornish version of Rumpelstiltskin has delightful twists. When the maid guesses the devil's name, everything that he has sewn turns to ashes. Lightly colored illustrations treat the story with grand humor, and at the instant the name is guessed, the Squire is left standing in the fields, naked except for hat and shoes.

HONORS

Three Jovial Huntsmen   Susan Jeffers   Bradbury

The three jovial huntsmen go a-hunting on St. David's day and find nothing they want. But lurking in the beautifully drawn forests, many animals are seen keeping a close watch on the huntsmen.

Cathedral   David Macaulay   Houghton

The single-mindedness and spirit of the people and their step-by-step construction of an imaginary medieval cathedral are meticulously recorded as the author-illustrator celebrates the lives and art of the craftsmen who built the magnificent Gothic cathedrals.

1973 AWARD

The Funny Little Woman   Retold by Arlene Mosel
Illustrated by Blair Lent   Dutton

A little woman pursues a rice dumpling and is led into the underground world of the wicked Oni. Her escape proves she is a funny little woman. Illustrations convey the mystery and humor of the strange world of the Oni as well as the dignity of this Japanese folktale.

HONORS

Hosie's Alphabet   Hosea, Tobias and Lisa Baskin
Illustrated by Leonard Baskin   Viking

From the bumptious baboon, to the primordial protozoa, right down to the "ruminating zebu," the artist presents an alphabet bestiary of ever-changing format where spiders' legs stretch across the page and dashes of watercolor become the eagle. This work is highly imaginative.

When Clay Sings   Byrd Baylor   Illustrated by Tom Bahti   Scribner

Illustrated with the designs found on prehistoric pottery from the American Southwest, this tribute to artifacts and those who used them evokes a reverence for an ancient way of life. The earth tones and prehistoric designs dignify the word images of the poetic text.

Snow-White and the Seven Dwarfs. A Tale from the Brothers Grimm
Translated by Randall Jarrell   Illustrated by Nancy Ekholm Burkert   Farrar

Strongly detailed illustrations in beautiful, soft colors evoke the sweeping, medieval, magical romance of fairy tales. Randall Jarrell translated the Brothers Grimm story of the beautiful girl, the wicked, malicious stepmother, and the sturdy, somber dwarfs.

Anansi the Spider: A Tale from the Ashanti
Adapted and illustrated by Gerald McDermott   Holt

> The moon is in the sky because Anansi, the great African folklore hero, could not decide which of his six sons should have it. Bright, geometric designs, bold, stylized animals, and rhythmic speech patterns are based on the Ashanti culture.

1972 AWARD

One Fine Day   Retold and illustrated by Nonny Hogrogian   Macmillan

Punished by having his tail cut off when he drank all the milk in an old woman's pail, the fox pleads to have it sewn back on so his friends won't make fun of him. The old woman agrees to do it, but only after he has returned her milk. The subdued and uncluttered pictures reflect the humorous cumulative action of the Armenian tale.

HONORS

If All the Seas Were One Sea   Janina Domanska   Macmillan

> An old nursery rhyme, its rise-and-fall rhythmic text reminiscent of the action of ocean waves, is treated to splendid etchings boldly filled with swirling, geometric lines of clear colors. The many shapes of each etching make a whole picture and provide the rhyme with even more momentum.

Moja Means One: Swahili Counting Book   Muriel Feelings
Illustrated by Tom Feelings   Dial

> Numbers from one to ten are represented by words in the Swahili language. Handsome, muted-gray double-page spread paintings depict scenes from Africa and relate to the illustrative sentences.

Hildilid's Night   Cheli Duran Ryan   Illustrated by Arnold Lobel   Macmillan

> Hildilid hates the night and the creatures of it. She does everything she can to chase the night away. Pen-and-ink drawings composed of thousands of tiny lines add a moonlit quality to the pages. Only at the end, with the approach of dawn, does yellow come into the picture.

1971 AWARD

A Story A Story   Retold and illustrated by Gail E. Haley   Atheneum

Kwaku Ananse, the great African spider man, completes three almost impossible tasks to win the Sky God's box of stories to tell throughout the world. The woodcut illustrations use African designs.

HONORS

Frog and Toad Are Friends   Arnold Lobel   Harper

In five affectionate and funny stories, best friends Frog and Toad share simple adventures and experiences. They welcome spring, find a lost button, tell stories, and enjoy being friends. The expressive and droll illustrations are in gray, frog green, and toad brown.

In the Night Kitchen   Maurice Sendak   Harper

Falling through the night and out of his clothes, Mickey lands in cake batter in the night kitchen. From there he goes to the dough, builds an airplane of it, and flies to the Milky Way. The dream-fantasy is carried out in a chanting rhyme and is illustrated with an adaptation of comic book art.

The Angry Moon   Retold by William Sleator   Illustrated by Blair Lent   Atlantic

A legend of the peoples of Alaska is retold with vigor, using lavish, full-color illustrations that elaborate on original Tlingit motifs. When Lapowinsa mocks the moon, she is taken into the sky country. Her friend must overcome many obstacles before he is able to rescue her.

1970 AWARD

Sylvester and the Magic Pebble   William Steig   Windmill

A collector of pebbles, Sylvester the donkey finds a magic one that grants wishes. Caught by a lion, Sylvester panics and wishes himself to be a rock. Full-color pictures show the seasonal changes and colorful characters of the story and extend its concern and gentle humor.

HONORS

Goggles!   Ezra Jack Keats   Macmillan

While showing off the motorcycle goggles he has found, Peter is accosted by neighborhood bullies. Proving that smart moves are more powerful than brute strength, Peter and his friends outwit the older boys. Rich, dark, brooding colors of paint and collage are lightened with vibrant colors in illustrations that reflect the urban setting.

Alexander and the Wind-Up Mouse   Leo Lionni   Pantheon

Alexander, an unappreciated house mouse, envies Willy the windup mouse because everyone loves and coddles him. After asking the wizard lizard to change him into a windup mouse, Alexander has a change of heart. Large, bold collages enhance the simply told story.

Pop Corn and Ma Goodness   Edna Mitchell Preston
Illustrated by Robert Andrew Parker   Viking

> With all the gaiety and drama of a folk song, this original story is told in nonsense verse. Ma Goodness and Pop Corn meet, fall in love, marry, build a house and a farm, have children, and enjoy the good life on their "prippitty proppetty." Watercolor pictures have a haphazard look that adds to the rollicking fun.

Thy Friend, Obadiah   Brinton Turkle   Viking

> His large Quaker family teases young Obadiah because a sea gull has taken a liking to him and follows him everywhere. The drawings are warm and gentle and vary greatly in perspective. When the sea gull fails to be seen for several days, Obadiah finds that what he thought was a nuisance is really a friend.

The Judge: An Untrue Tale   Harve Zemach
Illustrated by Margot Zemach   Farrar

> Prisoner after prisoner excitedly tells the Judge about the horrible thing that is on its way. The no-nonsense Judge throws them all in jail. When the horrible thing comes, poetic justice is done. Illustrated in watercolors and line drawings, the robust, pinkish characters tell their cumulative rhyming tale.

1969 AWARD

The Fool of the World and the Flying Ship   Retold by Arthur Ransome
Illustrated by Uri Shulevitz   Farrar

Line drawings and watercolors in bright, glowing, jewel-toned colors show the magnificent flying ship and the landscapes and onion domes of Russia. In this old Russian tale, the scorned and foolish younger son of peasants overcomes tremendous obstacles and wins the hand of the czar's daughter.

HONOR

Why the Sun and the Moon Live in the Sky   Elphinstone Dayrell
Illustrated by Blair Lent   Houghton

> Long ago, so the Nigerian folktale says, the Sun and Water were friends and lived on Earth together. When Sun invites Water to visit, the resulting flood forces them into the sky. Elaborately stylized African motifs and traditional patterns are used throughout the book.

1968 AWARD

Drummer Hoff   Barbara Emberley
Illustrated by Ed Emberley   Prentice-Hall

"Private Parridge brought the carriage," begins the cumulative text that leads to "Drummer Hoff fired it off" and a big "Kahbahblooom." Woodcuts show vibrantly colored old-fashioned military figures.

HONORS

Frederick   Leo Lionni   Pantheon

The other field mice scurry to gather food for winter while Frederick gathers warm thoughts. In the deep of winter when the food has run out, Frederick is called upon to share his supplies. Collages enhance this story that proves "we do not live by bread alone."

Seashore Story   Taro Yashima   Viking

On an island where "the quietness of ancient times" is felt, visiting children are reminded of the old story of Urashima, a fisherman who saved the life of a turtle. In return, the turtle takes him deep into the ocean to a mythical land. Muted pastel drawings capture the mysticism of the Japanese story.

The Emperor and the Kite   Jane Yolen   Illustrated by Ed Young   World

Djeow Seow was the smallest and least noticed of the emperor's children. When evil men come and snatch the emperor away, it is Djeow Seow and her kites who rescue him. Intricate paper cuttings provide great beauty and a sense of cultural heritage in this Japanese tale.

1967 AWARD

Sam, Bangs & Moonshine   Evaline Ness   Holt

Sam, a fisherman's daughter, has a bad habit of making up stories. The little girl learns to distinguish the truth from "moonshine" only after her best friend and her cat nearly meet tragedy. The book's pictures capture Sam's confusion of fact and fancy.

HONOR

One Wide River to Cross   Adapted by Barbara Emberley
Illustrated by Ed Emberley   Prentice-Hall

The text of an old folk song comes alive on brightly colored pages printed with black woodcuts. Stylized animals come forth one by one, two by two, and so on up to ten in nonsense verse with illustrations of animals that cumulate in groups waiting to board Noah's ark.

1963 AWARD

The Snowy Day   Ezra Jack Keats   Viking

Peter has fun on a snow-covered day making tracks and angels in the snow, building a snowman, and even trying to save a snowball for later. Spare, colorful collage pictures capture the wonder of a small child's trudge through new snow.

HONORS

The Sun Is a Golden Earring   Natalia M. Belting
Illustrated by Bernarda Bryson   Holt

People have always wondered about nature and have made up stories and sayings to explain natural phenomena. The author's collection of ancient sayings from folklore is reproduced here. The drawings lend an effective ethereal spirit to the book.

Mr. Rabbit and the Lovely Present   Charlotte Zolotow
Illustrated by Maurice Sendak   Harper

A little girl seeks birthday present advice from the wonderfully lanky, long-legged Mr. Rabbit. As the two wander through beautiful pastel scenes, she explains that her mother likes colors. They discuss many objects that are of the colors her mother likes the best.

1962 AWARD

Once a Mouse   Retold and illustrated by Marcia Brown   Scribner

The brief, carefully chosen text taken from a fable of ancient India tells of a hermit magician that changes a mouse into a cat, a dog, a tiger, and finally back into a mouse again. Illustrated in woodcuts filled with patterns, the overlaying of the gold, red, and black add even more dimension.

HONORS

The Day We Saw the Sun Come Up   Alice E. Goudey
Illustrated by Adrienne Adams   Scribner

In this poetic science book, two children get up very early in the morning and see the sun come up. They watch their long shadows and see what happens to them later in the day. Illustrations are in appropriate colors—gray and shadowy in the early morning, bright and clear at noon.

Little Bear's Visit   Else H. Minarik   Illustrated by Maurice Sendak   Harper

Little Bear thoroughly enjoys his visit with his grandparents and delights in the stories they tell. The brown, green, and black-and-white illustrations of the cuddly, loving Little Bear and his fully clothed grandparents are enhanced with fine crosshatching.

The Fox Went Out on a Chilly Night: An Old Song
Illustrated by Peter Spier   Doubleday

Alternating double-page spreads of full-color and black-and-white detailed drawings greatly extend the story told in the old song. The fox kills a duck and a goose, outruns the farmer, and dines with his wife with fork and knife while the ten little pups chew on the "bones-o." The musical score is appended.

1961 AWARD

Baboushka and the Three Kings   Ruth Robbins
Illustrated by Nicolas Sidjakov   Parnassus

Old Baboushka declined to go with the three kings in search of the Child. Now, every year at Christmastime she continues her endless, endless search. On her way she leaves gifts for children. Rich, four-color, angular pictures in primitive style adorn the Russian tale.

HONOR

Inch by Inch   Leo Lionni   Obolensky

An inchworm saves himself from being eaten because he is able to measure things—a robin's tail, a flamingo's neck, a humming bird's body. But when asked to measure the nightingale's song, the inchworm must think fast. The bright green inchworm inches its way out of sight through a collage of grass.

1960 AWARD

Nine Days to Christmas   Marie Hall Ets and Aurora Labastida
Illustrated by Marie Hall Ets   Viking

Now that she is in kindergarten, Ceci is old enough to join in the posadas—part of the special Christmas celebration that begins nine days before Christmas. Anticipation mounts as Ceci chooses her own piñata. Soft, gray backgrounds with splashes of bright colors project the warmth and excitement of the Mexican tradition in an urban setting.

HONORS

Houses from the Sea   Alice E. Goudey
Illustrated by Adrienne Adams   Scribner

> Soft watercolor washes combine with poetic text to set the tone of this quiet, informative story. Two children gather shells along the coast and talk about the various shapes of the shells. An introduction and afterword provide more scientific information.

The Moon Jumpers   Janice May Udry   Illustrated by Maurice Sendak   Harper

> When the sun goes down, the moon comes up. Four children calling themselves the moon jumpers joyfully play and dance under the moonlit sky before bedtime. Soft night colors add a mystic touch to the simple story.

1959 AWARD

Chanticleer and the Fox   Adapted from Chaucer's Canterbury Tales
Illustrated by Barbara Cooney   Crowell

The old fable of the proud rooster and the wily fox was retold by Chaucer in his *Canterbury Tales*. Cooney has adapted that version for children. The text is filled with descriptive language, while the illustrations, rich in color and strong lines, capture medieval times.

HONORS

The House That Jack Built: La Maison Que Jacques A Batie
Antonio Frasconi   Harcourt

> An old cumulative nursery rhyme, told in English and French, is illustrated with brilliantly colored woodcuts. A review at the end of the text asks questions in English and provides answers in French.

What Do You Say, Dear?   Sesyle Joslin
Illustrated by Maurice Sendak   W. R. Scott

> Absurdly funny and outlandish situations are presented, followed by the question, "what do you say, dear?" and the proper rule of etiquette. Blue, yellow, and black illustrations continue the hilarity, even though the rule is presented straightforwardly.

Umbrella   Taro Yashima   Viking

> Thrilled with the umbrella and red boots she receives on her third birthday, Momo impatiently waits out the days until it rains. How proud she is when she can finally use her new rain gear! The impressionistic illustrations are filled with brush strokes of red, blues, and yellows and reflect the Japanese culture.

1958 AWARD

Time of Wonder   Robert McCloskey   Viking

McCloskey celebrates in prose and painting the island where he lives. The alternately quiet and boisterous moods of nature are peacefully or dramatically recounted. The children of the island explore and enjoy the changing moods as the intensity of the blue and green watercolors shifts with the changes in the weather.

HONORS

Fly High, Fly Low   Don Freeman   Viking

In a story of love, loyalty, and suspense, the pigeon Sid faces perils while searching for the missing Midge, their nest, and the big letter B where their nest is housed. Colorful illustrations reveal scenes of San Francisco.

Anatole and the Cat   Eve Titus   Illustrated by Paul Galdone   McGraw-Hill

Mouse Anatole, a loving husband and caring father, bicycles through the streets of Paris each night on his way to work. When a cat arrives on the scene, Anatole succeeds where thousands of other mice have failed. Gray drawings with accents of red, white, and blue and a smattering of French words reinforce the setting of the story.

1957 AWARD

A Tree Is Nice   Janice Udry   Illustrated by Marc Simont   Harper

Trees are wonderful: They give shade, are fun to climb, are great to swing from, and even give cats a place to hide from dogs. Illustrated with watercolors, this book is a celebration of trees.

HONORS

Gillespie and the Guards   Benjamin Elkin
Illustrated by James Daugherty   Viking

Gillespie sets out to fool the three haughty guards by the old trick of the obvious. Robust illustrations are filled with humor and point with pride to the little boy who outsmarts the smug guards.

Lion   William Pène du Bois   Viking

High in the sky, in the place where animals are invented, the boss comes up with a wonderful new name for an animal—"lion." His difficulty in deciding what it should look like is depicted in a line drawing of his original idea of a lion, complete with feathers, fur, and fish scales.

Mr. Penny's Race Horse   Marie Hall Ets   Viking

Mr. Penny promises his animals a ride on the Ferris wheel if they win enough prize money at the fair. In an attempt to make sure they win first prize, the animals cause chaos. The dark black-and-white illustrations of the farm and the fair are all set within a border.

Anatole   Eve Titus   Illustrated by Paul Galdone   McGraw-Hill

Shocked and shaken when he overhears humans saying that mice are terrible and dirty, Anatole the mouse determines to give humans something in return for the food he takes. Red, white, blue, and gray illustrations alternate with black-and-white ones as they reveal the world from the perspective of a French mouse.

1 Is One   Tasha Tudor   Walck

Simple verse and delicate old-fashioned paintings and drawings introduce numerals from one to twenty. Each page is bordered with charming drawings of wild flowers. Within the borders children and scenes from nature represent the number depicted.

1956 AWARD

Frog Went A-Courtin'   Retold by John Langstaff
Illustrated by Feodor Rojankovsky   Harcourt

In this story based on an old song and written in snappy, rhyming couplets, a frog courts Miss Mousie, and soon the insects and small animals scurry about preparing for the wedding feast. Full-color illustrations alternate with black-and-white and frog green ones, climaxing in a state of confusion as the cat joins the feast. Music is included.

HONORS

Play with Me   Marie Hall Ets   Viking

Reaching out to touch the woodland animals that she wants to play with, the little girl finds that they all run from her. She sits very still, and one by one the animals come close to her. Repetition in the story is loosely carried out in the quiet drawings as the girl never strays far from the pond.

Crow Boy   Taro Yashima   Viking

In a deeply sensitive school story, Chibi, a very shy boy, is taunted by his classmates for years. A new teacher takes the time to talk to Chibi and discovers his talents. Set in a Japanese village, the story is illustrated with brush strokes that reflect an economy of style.

1955 AWARD

Cinderella, or the Little Glass Slipper
Illustrated and translated from Charles Perrault
by Marcia Brown   Scribner

Freely translated from Charles Perrault's French tale, this story of Cinderella, her ugly stepsisters, the fairy godmother, and the glass slipper is enhanced with illustrations that fairly dance across the pages with pink and aqua colors and whispy black lines. The enchanting pictures capture the romance of the tale.

HONORS

Wheel on the Chimney   Margaret Wise Brown
Illustrated by Tibor Gergely   Lippincott

> Storks come from Africa to build their nest on the chimney and live by the cool, green rivers of Hungary. When fall comes they fly south over towns, rivers, and bridges. The full-page paintings of the Mediterranean city, the pink flamingos, and the flock of white storks in flight are striking in color.

The Thanksgiving Story   Alice Dalgliesh   Illustrated by Helen Sewell   Scribner

> Events leading up to the first Thanksgiving celebration in Plymouth Colony are told with the Hopkins family as the focus. Flat, primitive color illustrations of people are interspersed with rust-colored silhouettes of objects important to the Pilgrims in their new land.

Book of Nursery and Mother Goose Rhymes   Illustrated by Marguerite de Angeli
Doubleday

> Three hundred seventy-six rhymes are delicately illustrated in this oversized book. A soft, cheerful tone pervades the sketches, many of which were inspired by scenes of the English countryside. A small sketch of a goose appears on almost every page.

1954 AWARD

Madeline's Rescue   Ludwig Bemelmans   Viking

When Madeline is rescued from the river by a dog, the dog becomes the heroine of the convent school. The girls love the dog, but the trustees say it must go. Bright, irrepressible pictures match the indomitable spirit of the little French girl.

HONORS

The Steadfast Tin Soldier   Hans Christian Andersen, translated by M. R. James
Illustrated by Marcia Brown   Scribner

> Five-and-twenty tin soldiers, all made from the same tin spoon, look alike except for the last one made. He stands firmly on his one leg. It is he who falls in love with the toy ballerina. Their tragic story is enhanced with blue-violet and red drawings.

Green Eyes   A. Birnbaum   Capitol

> An all-white cat with long whiskers and green eyes is about to celebrate his first birthday. In simple text and drawings reminiscent of the bold lines of children's art, the tale of Green Eyes's activities in the four seasons that have just passed unfolds.

A Very Special House   Ruth Krauss   Illustrated by Maurice Sendak   Harper

> The little boy is blissfully happy as he tells of a house he knows where he puts his feet on the table, bounces on the bed, and swings on the door. It is a place where everyone yells for more, and no one ever says "stop." Line illustrations seem to frolic across the page, and only at the end is it revealed that the story is a triumph of imaginary play.

Journey Cake, Ho!   Ruth Sawyer   Illustrated by Robert McCloskey   Viking

> When there is only enough food left to feed two, not three, the bound-out boy is sent on his way with a huge Journey Cake. The cake breaks free, bounces down the road, and soon animal after animal joins the chase until they all end up where the boy started. Expressive illustrations provide the feel of an American folktale.

When Will the World Be Mine? Miriam Schlein
Illustrated by Jean Charlot   W. R. Scott

> Little Snowshoe Rabbit is born in the spring. His mother spends much of the year protecting and teaching him. She gently shows him how to adapt to the world around him, and in that way the world becomes his. The lithographs in browns and greens show stylized rabbits and their view of the world.

1953 AWARD

The Biggest Bear   Lynd Ward   Houghton

Humiliated because his family has the only barn that never has a bear skin hanging on it, Johnny sets out with his shotgun in search of a bear. He returns home with a live, cuddly, hungry bear cub that soon grows into a big, rambunctious, voracious bear. The illustrations are sensitive, strong, and robust.

HONORS

Ape in a Cape: An Alphabet of Odd Animals   Fritz Eichenberg   Harcourt

Bold, humorous, colorful pictures and short, nonsense verses combine to create a lively alphabet book. From the "bear in despair" to the "yak with a pack," there is wonderful fun and imagination on each page.

Five Little Monkeys   Juliet Kepes   Houghton

Buzzo, Binki, Bulu, Bibi, and Bali are the little mischievous monkeys who, because of their irritating tricks, cause the other jungle animals to band together to punish them. Alternating pages of color and black-and-white illustrations show the stylized monkeys acting up.

One Morning in Maine   Robert McCloskey   Viking

While clam digging with her father, Sally loses a tooth that falls amongst the pebbles of the beach. Large, dark blue lithographs depict the great pride associated with losing the first baby tooth. All the characters in the small Maine town enjoy Sally's joy.

Puss in Boots   Illustrated and translated from Charles Perrault
by Marcia Brown   Scribner

The youngest son inherits a cat and realizes that after eating it he will have nothing left. Crafty Puss in Boots tells his master to do as he says and all will be well, and indeed it is! Puss, with his fine red boots, is shown as a grand, swashbuckling character who takes command of all the folderol of a French court.

The Storm Book   Charlotte Zolotow
Illustrated by Margaret Bloy Graham   Harper

A little boy watches in wonder as the day turns ominously gray and still, a storm approaches, and breaks forth. He asks his mother questions and she replies with reassuring answers. Each two-page spread of text is followed by a double-page spread of illustrations, most of them showing a driving rain.

1952 AWARD

Finders Keepers   Will, pseud. (William Lipkind)
Illustrated by Nicolas, pseud. (Nicolas Mordvinoff)   Harcourt

Two dogs find a bone. One saw it first; the other touched it first. Unable to decide who owns it, they bury it and go off to seek the opinion of others and in so doing almost lose the bone to another dog. The bold use of color adds spark and flair to the simple story.

HONORS

Skipper John's Cook   Marcia Brown   Scribner

Beans! That was the trouble. The Skipper's crew refuses to sign on until a cook is found who does not fix beans morning, noon, and night. Young Si is hired on. After he has fried his 259th fish, the crew wants to know what else he can cook. Beans! Illustrations capture the expressions of the crew—and of the pots and pans.

Bear Party   William Pène du Bois   Viking

When the koala bears become very angry with each other, it is "the wise old bear who lives at the top of the tallest Eucalyptus tree" who decides what to do. The koala bears are shown dressed in all the finery of a masked costume party, while wonderful onomatopoeic words describe the sounds of the musical instruments.

Mr. T. W. Anthony Woo   Marie Hall Ets   Viking

Pandemonium reigns at the cobbler's when his dog and cat fight each other, and then both chase Mr. T. W. Anthony Woo, the mouse. Sister and her parrot move in, and things go from bad to worse until the enemies band together to create peace. Illustrations are contained within borders and suggest the control the cobbler wishes he had.

Feather Mountain   Elizabeth Olds   Houghton

At one time all birds were naked and pink and featherless. One day they ask the Great Spirit to give them coverings. Black-and-white and color pictures depict the birds as they scurry around finding just the right colors to blend with their habitats.

All Falling Down   Gene Zion   Illustrated by Margaret Bloy Graham   Harper

So many things fall—petals, rain, apples, even Daddy's book when his head begins to nod. This quiet, reflective book is illustrated with pastel colors. There is a surprise ending when Daddy tosses the baby in the air.

1951 AWARD

The Egg Tree   Katherine Milhous   Scribner

An Easter morning egg hunt leads to the discovery of long forgotten decorated eggs. With them the family begins a new tradition. Pennsylvania Dutch folk designs border many of the pages; the colors found in hex signs dominate the paintings that interpret the story.

HONORS

Dick Whittington and His Cat   Marcia Brown   Scribner

Artistic linoleum block cuts have humor and charm. They illustrate a simple retelling of the folktale of the boy who was made wealthy because he listened to his cat.

If I Ran the Zoo   Dr. Seuss, pseud. (Theodor Seuss Geisel)   Random House

Young Gerald McGrew likes the zoo but knows that if he ran it he would make some changes. He imagines all kinds of fantastic beasts with wonderfully creative names and unusual shapes and habits. Zany, whimsical illustrations are perfect for the imaginative verse.

The Two Reds   Will, pseud. (William Lipkind)
Illustrated by Nicolas, pseud. (Nicolas Mordvinoff)   Harcourt

Red, the boy, sets out to play at the same time Red, an independent cat, sets out for food. The sense of impending chaos mounts as each gets in trouble at the same time in different parts of town. Sparse line drawings with brilliant splashes of red add spark to the illustrations.

T-Bone, the Baby Sitter   Clare Turlay Newberry   Harper

T-Bone the cat loves to sit. That is what makes him such a fine baby-sitter—until the day he awakens with a twinkle in his eye, full of mischief. Expressive illustrations show the baby's extreme displeasure when T-Bone is taken away to the country and his pleasure when he returns.

The Most Wonderful Doll in the World   Phyllis McGinley
Illustrated by Helen Stone   Lippincott

Duley loses a new doll. Her imagination runs wild as she describes the lost and most wonderful doll in the world as she wants it to be, not as it is. The book is decorated with four-color and black-and-white illustrations and borders.

1950 AWARD

Song of the Swallows   Leo Politi   Scribner

The bell ringer and gardener of the mission church in Capistrano tells Juan the history of the mission churches and of the return of the swallows every St. Joseph's Day. Pinks, grays, yellows, and greens in muted tones convey friendship and a respect for nature. Two songs are included in the text.

HONORS

Henry Fisherman   Marcia Brown   Scribner

> To be a fisherman a boy has to be able to swim very fast in case a shark is near. As the day when Juan will be allowed on the fishing boat draws closer, sights and sounds of a childhood in the Virgin Islands are portrayed in brown, coral, yellow, and green.

The Wild Birthday Cake   Lavinia R. Davis
Illustrated by Hildegard Woodward   Doubleday

> Johnny is so excited about going on an adventurous hike that he almost forgets his friend's seventy-fifth birthday. On his hike he catches a wild duck and later gives it to his friend as a gift. Abundant on the pages are the yellows and greens of spring.

Bartholomew and the Oobleck
Dr. Seuss, pseud. (Theodor Seuss Geisel)   Random House

> Tired of snow, fog, rain, and sunshine, the king wants something new to fall from the sky. What he gets are green, gooey globs of oobleck that threaten to destroy the kingdom. Comical illustrations in black-and-white become greener and greener as the oobleck spreads.

America's Ethan Allen   Stewart Holbrook   Illustrated by Lynd Ward   Houghton

> Brave and rebellious Ethan Allen is born in the wilds of the old colony of Connecticut. He grows into a rugged frontier hero who leads the Green Mountain Boys. The illustrations and writing style resound with patriotism and historical significance.

The Happy Day   Ruth Krauss   Illustrated by Marc Simont   Harper

> The woodland animals are all in their winter's sleep when something causes them to open their eyes and sniff. Suspense mounts as they all race toward the thing that has caused them to awaken. Black-and-white drawings portray joyous animals as they leap around a bright yellow flower—the first sign of spring and the only color in the book.

1949 AWARD

The Big Snow   Berta and Elmer Hader   Macmillan

When they see the wild geese flying overhead, all the woodland animals scurry to get ready for winter. After the big snow they slowly emerge to find food. Black-and-white drawings are occasionally interspersed with full-color paintings.

HONORS

Blueberries for Sal   Robert McCloskey   Viking

On the same day that Little Sal and her mother go to Blueberry Hill to pick blueberries, so do Little Bear and his mother. Soon a mix-up in mothers occurs. Dark blue-and-white type and drawings promote gentle humor against the ruggedness of Blueberry Hill.

All Around the Town   Phyllis McGinley   Illustrated by Helen Stone   Lippincott

Snappy rhythm of the text and splashes of color in the illustrations capture the gaiety and pace of city life. Each verse is about a city sight and the rhymes are arranged in alphabetical order, from Aeroplane to Zoo.

Juanita   Leo Politi   Scribner

As Easter draws near, Juanita and her friends join in the parade for the Blessing of the Animals at the Old Mission Church. The text is lovingly illustrated and interspersed with some songs, making the warmth of a close-knit community in old Los Angeles come alive.

Fish in the Air   Kurt Wiese   Viking

On their way to fly a great big kite, Fish and his kite are grabbed by a Tai Fung, or big wind. It sends them on a high-flying adventure. Colorful paintings portray the excitement caused when Fish flies over town and countryside.

1948 AWARD

White Snow, Bright Snow   Alvin Tresselt
Illustrated by Roger Duvoisin   Lothrop

Slowly the snow begins to fall and the adults busy themselves preparing for it. The children revel in it. A dark blue background gives way to white as the heavy snow melts and spring breaks forth. Reds and yellows provide a cheerful balance.

HONORS

Stone Soup   Marcia Brown   Scribner

An inhospitable town refuses to help three hungry soldiers. When the soldiers decide to make a soup of stones, curiosity overcomes the peasants and they learn a lesson in cooperation. Orange and brown pictures portray peasant life in a long-ago French village.

Roger and the Fox   Lavinia R. Davis
Illustrated by Hildegard Woodward   Doubleday

> Roger wants to see the wild fox and tries many times before he figures out how to be quick and quiet enough to do it. The pictures turn from the warm hues of fall to the cold blues of winter before patience and ingenuity finally pay off.

McElligot's Pool   Dr. Seuss, pseud. (Theodor Seuss Geisel)   Random House

> Told that he is some sort of fool for trying to catch fish in McElligot's pool, Marco visualizes the possibility that the pool is connected to the sea. Wonderfully imaginative creatures with fantastic names swim across the pages of this story told in verse.

Song of Robin Hood   Edited by Anne Malcolmson
Designed and illustrated by Virginia Lee Burton   Houghton

> Eighteen ballads of Robin Hood, most traced back to their original tunes, are exuberantly presented in verse, music, and art. The five hundred verses are decorated in a style reminiscent of miniature drawings of the fifteenth century. Its words meant to be sung not read, the book provides an energetic and lyrical introduction to the famous Robin Hood.

Bambino the Clown   Georges Schreiber   Viking

> The full colors and excitement of a circus clown's act are experienced by a sad young boy whom Bambino befriends. Peter is invited into the clown's dressing room, watches him apply his makeup, and becomes a very funny part of the show.

1947 AWARD

The Little Island   Golden MacDonald, pseud. (Margaret Wise Brown)
Illustrated by Leonard Weisgard   Doubleday

The seasons come and go and little by little the small island changes. One day a kitten visits the island and discovers that it does not stand alone but is connected underwater to land. The moods of the mostly green and blue drawings change with the seasons.

HONORS

Boats on the River   Marjorie Flack   Illustrated by Jay Hyde Barnum   Viking

> There are warships, ocean liners, rowboats, and many other boats on the river that flows by the city and out to sea. Full-color paintings show close and distant views of the boats.

Timothy Turtle   Al Graham   Illustrated by Tony Palazzo   Welch

On the day Timothy flips over on his back, each animal tries to help him right himself. The wise frog tells the other animals that what they could not do as individuals they can do as a group. Action-packed drawings add tautness and humor to the tale.

Pedro, the Angel of Olvera Street   Leo Politi   Scribner

Young Pedro, who sings like an angel, leads La Posada, the Christmas procession, on Olvera Street in Los Angeles. For nine consecutive nights he wears red wings and sings carols of Christian pilgrims. The soft colors reflect the solemnity of the procession. Music is included.

Rain Drop Splash   Alvin Tresselt   Illustrated by Leonard Weisgard   Lothrop

A single rain drop splashes down. Soon it is joined by others, and a puddle is formed. The puddle grows bigger and bigger until the rain drops at last become the sea, and the rain stops. The poetic patterns of the text and the drenched look of the pictures provide a closeness to nature.

Sing in Praise: A Collection of the Best Loved Hymns   Opal Wheeler
Illustrated by Marjorie Torrey   Dutton

Twenty-five perennially popular Christian hymns have been arranged to simple piano scores. Most of the hymns are accompanied by a laudatory story about how the particular words or melody came to be written. Romanticized illustrations show pious children looking heavenward.

1946 AWARD

The Rooster Crows   Maud and Miska Petersham   Macmillan

A potpourri of the rhymes, jingles, and chants of American children is treated to a variety of visual interpretations. Each rhyme is illustrated with humor and rhythm.

HONORS

Little Lost Lamb   Golden MacDonald, pseud. (Margaret Wise Brown)
Illustrated by Leonard Weisgard   Doubleday

When the little black lamb strays from the rest of the flock, the little shepherd and his sheepdog go into the perilous night in search of it. The mood of the story changes from bright, frolicsome pictures of the frisky lamb to dark browns that reflect the concern the boy has for the lost animal.

My Mother Is the Most Beautiful Woman in the World   Becky Reyher
Illustrated by Ruth Gannett   Lothrop

> When a little girl becomes lost, she describes her mother with her heart not with her eyes. Colorful pictures reflect the spirit of the old Russian proverb, "We do not love people because they are beautiful, but they seem beautiful to us because we love them."

Sing Mother Goose   Music by Opal Wheeler
Illustrated by Marjorie Torrey   Dutton

> Fifty-two of the most familiar Mother Goose nursery rhymes have been arranged to original, sprightly music. The piano scores and the rhymes are accompanied by illustrations of children, many of whom are in late-Victorian dress.

You Can Write Chinese   Kurt Wiese   Viking

> In China in the 1940s, a classroom of boys receives a language lesson. The teacher explains that there are no letters in the Chinese language, only words based on ancient pictures. Most of the book consists of large drawings of Chinese characters superimposed on drawings of objects that represent the words.

1945 AWARD

Prayer for a Child   Rachel Field
Illustrated by Elizabeth Orton Jones   Macmillan

A child's bedtime prayer asks for blessings on things that are familiar to small children with such lines as, "Bless other children, far and near, And keep them safe and free from fear." Brief lines of the prayer are illustrated with full-page, reverent golden-toned drawings.

HONORS

In the Forest   Marie Hall Ets   Viking

> With his new horn and paper hat a little boy takes a walk in the forest, and along the way he meets storks, kangaroos, bears, and other animals who join his parade. All disappear when the boy's father comes hunting for him. There is a strong contrast between the white figures and the black forest backgrounds.

Yonie Wondernose   Marguerite de Angeli   Doubleday

> His father has promised him something very special as soon as seven-year-old Yonie learns to handle responsibilities like a man. Strongly depicted in the illustrations and the text is the hard but cheerful way of life on an Amish farm.

The Christmas Anna Angel   Ruth Sawyer   Illustrated by Kate Seredy   Viking

In a story set in Hungary during the war, Anna longs for a Christmas cake shaped like a little clock. The deprivations caused by the war contrast with the happy family traditions of Christmas. While heavy on text, the book has several illustrations reflective of the folk culture.

Mother Goose   Illustrated by Tasha Tudor   Oxford University Press

Seventy-seven Mother Goose rhymes are gathered together in this small book. Many of the rhymes are familiar, but some are those usually found only in complete works. Quaint, soft-colored pictures abound on every page.

1944 AWARD

Many Moons   James Thurber   Illustrated by Louis Slobodkin   Harcourt

After eating too many raspberry tarts, the princess declares that if she can have the moon she will be well again. The wisdom of the royal advisors fails. The common sense of the jester prevails. Washes of pinks and blues complement the whimsy of the humorous fantasy.

HONORS

A Child's Good Night Book   Margaret Wise Brown
Illustrated by Jean Charlot   W. R. Scott

Night has come and everything is going to sleep. Animals, children, and even engines are sleepy. The brief story ends with a prayer to bless and guard "small things that have no words." The repetitious phrases and drawings are designed to bring on drowsiness.

Good-Luck Horse   Chih-Yi Chan   Illustrated by Plato Chan   Whittlesey

A lonely boy in ancient China creates a very small paper horse that he can hold in his hand. Magically the horse becomes real. Although the magician names it "Good-Luck Horse," the story proves that sometimes good luck is bad luck and vice versa. The adventures of the horse are re-created in the line and wash drawings.

The Mighty Hunter   Berta and Elmer Hader   Macmillan

Little Brave Heart's mother tells him to go to school so he can grow up to be a wise leader, but he goes hunting instead. Each animal in turn tells him that there is a better animal to shoot. The bear chastises him for hunting for "fun," and chases him to school. The illustrations alternate between black-and-white and desert colors.

Small Rain: Verses from the Bible   Verses selected by Jessie Orton Jones
Illustrated by Elizabeth Orton Jones   Viking

> Brief Bible verses taken from the King James Version of the Old and New Testaments are illustrated with children doing everyday things—romping, playing, sitting quietly, sharing, running, crying, and sleeping. Each verse relates in some way to what the children are doing.

Pierre Pigeon   Lee Kingman   Illustrated by Arnold E. Bare   Houghton

> Seven-year-old Pierre has long been fascinated by the boat-in-bottle in the shop. Finally he purchases it, and before he gets it home he breaks it. Studying the broken model, he succeeds in figuring out how the boat got into the bottle. Gray, green, and peach tones reflect a Canadian fishing village.

1943 AWARD

The Little House   Virginia Lee Burton   Houghton

Built long ago far out in the country, the Little House is now surrounded by the city. Circular shapes abound in the illustrations and the lines of type. Bright, happy colors give way to dark, moody ones as progress overtakes the house. Light colors return when the house is moved to a new countryside.

HONORS

Dash and Dart   Mary and Conrad Buff   Viking

> In simple, poetic text and mood-capturing sepia paintings, the first year in the life of two fawns is described. A great reverence for nature is felt throughout the book.

Marshmallow   Clare Turlay Newberry   Harper

> Oliver the cat lives a blissful life of eating and sleeping until the lady who takes care of him brings home a bundle of live, soft fur. Suddenly Oliver is terrified when he is confronted with a bunny named Marshmallow. The pictures show how their relationship grows until they both curl up together.

1942 AWARD

Make Way for Ducklings   Robert McCloskey   Viking

Having hatched her ducklings and taught them to march nicely in single file, Mrs. Mallard decides to take them straight through Boston's busy streets to their new home in the Public Garden and pond. Sketchy brown drawings humorously show the ordeal the mallards face.

HONORS

In My Mother's House   Ann Nolan Clark
Illustrated by Velino Herrera   Viking

>Daily life of the pueblo as seen through the eyes of the children is described in a rhythmic, simple prose. Many aspects of life—houses, food, clothing, and agriculture—are pictured. Tribal designs and pen-and-ink and color drawings depict the Tawa life.

Nothing at All   Wanda Gág   Coward

>Three orphan dogs, two visible and one invisible, are adopted by two children. It takes a jackdaw, some magic, and a lot of energetic work by Nothing At All to become Something After All. Intriguing, lightly colored lithographs show the invisible become visible.

Paddle-to-the-Sea   Holling C. Holling   Houghton

>In the Canadian wilderness, a young boy carves a canoe with an Indian figure seated in it, then launches it from Lake Nipigon. The text and illustrations are filled with information about the scenes the canoe passes, from the quiet byways, to a sawmill, to a raging forest fire.

An American ABC   Maud and Miska Petersham   Macmillan

>Familiar symbols, historic places, and legendary figures form the basis of this patriotic interpretation of the alphabet. Decorated in red, white, blue, and black, each letter provides a brief lesson in American history. The strength and courage of those who shaped America are visible in the drawings.

1941 AWARD

They Were Strong and Good   Robert Lawson   Viking

Writing of his mother and father and their mothers and fathers, Lawson says they, like the ancestors of many others, were never famous but were "strong and good" and helped to build America. Line-and-brush drawings are sometimes humorous but more often depict the strength and goodness of the land and its people.

HONOR

April's Kittens   Clare Turlay Newberry   Harper

>After her cat has kittens, April must decide on the one cat to keep. Illustrations of the black cats make them look fuzzy and furry. Occasional touches of red add a dash of color.

1940 AWARD

Abraham Lincoln   Ingri and Edgar Parin d'Aulaire   Doubleday

Well-known anecdotes of Lincoln, particularly of his youth and prairie years, are recounted with strength and humor in this picture biography. Lithographs in color and black and white reveal details of American life in the 1800s.

HONORS

Madeline   Ludwig Bemelmans   Viking

High-spirited Madeline may be the smallest of the twelve little girls at Miss Clavel's school, but she is by far the bravest. Lilting rhythmic text and simple, childlike paintings provide a tour of Paris and introduce a spunky heroine.

The Ageless Story   Illustrated by Lauren Ford   Dodd

The story of the Christ Child is told through Gregorian music, biblical text, and illustrations that are an adaptation of illuminated manuscripts. The illustrations are a blend of early Renaissance religious art in a New England setting.

Cock-a-Doodle-Doo   Berta and Elmer Hader   Macmillan

In a reversal of the story of the Ugly Duckling, a chick is hatched by a duck. The ducklings make fun of him, and soon the chick goes off in search of others like him. In alternating color and black-and-white pictures he faces several perils before landing in the hen house.

1939 AWARD

Mei Li   Thomas Handforth   Doubleday

The New Year Fair is in the city, and Mei Li's brother has been told that he can go, but little girls have to stay home. Strong, bold line drawings present many aspects of Chinese culture and customs as they follow the irrepressible Mei Li, who sneaks off for a grand time at the fair.

HONORS

The Forest Pool   Laura Adams Armer   Longmans

Glowing with the bright golden colors of South America, stylized pictures show two boys as they go in search of the iguana in the bell-flower tree. The boys ponder the animals that know so much but never reveal their secrets.

Andy and the Lion   James Daugherty   Viking

The old story of Androcles and the lion is retold in a modern setting. Andy signs out a book about lions from the library. The next day he comes upon a lion with a thorn stuck in his paw. Told and illustrated with robust tall-tale humor, the twists of the tale lead to a fine friendship.

Snow White and the Seven Dwarfs
Translated and illustrated by Wanda Gág   Coward

In this little book the Brothers Grimm story of the vain, wicked stepmother, the seven dwarfs, and the beautiful princess is retold with much repetition. The black-and-white drawings are filled with rounded shapes that continue the repetitiousness of the story.

Wee Gillis   Munro Leaf   Illustrated by Robert Lawson   Viking

The Highland relatives want Wee Gillis to stalk stags with them. The Lowland relatives want him to tend the cows. After years of doing both, Wee Gillis has powerful lungs from calling the cows, and he has learned to sit very still from stalking stags—just the skills needed to play a bagpipe! Line drawings sparkle with humorous spirit.

Barkis   Clare Turlay Newberry   Harper

A bickering brother and sister squabble over the ownership of a new puppy and cat. They finally reach a solution that makes them both happy. Soft brown-and-black drawings of the winsome cat and dog are set against white backgrounds.

1938 AWARD

Animals of the Bible, a Picture Book   Text selected by Helen Dean Fish
Illustrated by Dorothy P. Lathrop   Lippincott

The Old and New Testaments of the King James Version are the sources for thirty-one stories about animals. Black-and-white full-page illustrations include the flora of biblical lands and portray the animals with reverence.

HONORS

Seven Simeons: A Russian Tale
Retold and illustrated by Boris Artzybasheff   Viking

King Douda, wise, rich, strong, and very handsome, decides to marry a princess as beautiful as himself. To help him in his quest, he engages seven brothers, each of whom has a special skill that, by the tale's end, is used in a most unusual manner. Love triumphs in the end in this whimsically decorated book with neat color line drawings.

Four and Twenty Blackbirds   Compiled by Helen Dean Fish
Illustrated by Robert Lawson   Stokes

The twenty-four nursery rhymes found here were culled from out-of-print books or "rescued from memories of older people." Most are long and filled with the jingling and sturdy humor of traditional nursery rhymes. They are illustrated with vigorous drawings in black and green. Simple music is given for those rhymes that have tunes.

The Media Used in Caldecott Picture Books
Notes toward a Definitive List

Christine Behrmann

Since 1938 more than one hundred artists have illustrated picture books that have won a Caldecott Award or been named Caldecott Honor Books. Each of these books has won the accolade because of the quality of its illustrator's distinctive style, a style that has evoked images and ideas in the reader's mind that remain long after the book is closed. As the book is reviewed and discussed, we talk much about the artist's imagination, talent, and unique eye. Mentioned less often is the physical process by which the images imagined by that unique eye come to life and the role of the artist's medium (paint, lithography, pen and ink, etc.) in that process. In the fifty years since the Caldecott Award was first given, there has apparently been no systematic attempt to list the media used to create the honored picture books. This is a loss, because it is scholarly information useful to the study of children's literature, and because it is a humbling and educating experience to see the care, skill, and sheer craftsmanship that go into the creation of a truly distinguished picture book. This article is an initial attempt to fill the void.

What follows must be a work in progress, as digging out this information is a process that involves not only library research, but also correspondence with the artist, editor, or art director, and with other collections. In some cases, the information may be lost forever because it was never written down in bibliographic descriptions, and the author and the publisher are no longer available to be questioned. It is heartening to note that some publishers, such as Dial and Greenwillow, are beginning

Reprinted, with changes, from *Journal of Youth Services in Libraries* (winter 1988): 198–212. Christine Behrmann was Children's Materials Specialist, Office of Children's Services, New York Public Library.

to list—in the books themselves—the media used in creating the pictures. This practice will certainly aid in the appreciation of the picture book as art.

The data listed below are thus, in many cases, preliminary only. Guesses were not made. When hard data were not found, the entry was left blank, except for a question mark. No information was regarded as final unless it was found in two independent secondary sources (review, bibliography, catalog, etc.) or available from one primary source (book, artist, publisher, Caldecott citation). Information from only one secondary source was included but marked preliminary by a question mark in parentheses. Corrections and added information are earnestly solicited. The most important result is to obtain, eventually, a complete, accurate list.

Many deserve thanks for their kind cooperation thus far, but it is most important to single out Lyn Lacey, whose excellent idea this project was.

1938 / WINNER

Animals of the Bible by Helen Dean Fish; Illustrated by Dorothy P. Lathrop (Lippincott)—black-and-white lithographs

HONORS

Seven Simeons by Boris Artzybasheff (Viking)—pen and ink

Four and Twenty Blackbirds by Helen Dean Fish; Illustrated by Robert Lawson (Stokes)—drawings in pen and tempera

1939 / WINNER

Mei Li by Thomas Handforth (Doubleday)—brush and lithograph pencil (?)

HONORS

The Forest Pool by Laura Adams Armer (Longmans)—medium not known

Wee Gillis by Munro Leaf; Illustrated by Robert Lawson (Viking)—drawings in pen and tempera

Snow White and the Seven Dwarfs by Wanda Gág (Coward)—lithographs (?)

Barkis by Clare Newberry (Harper)—charcoal pencil and watercolor wash

Andy and the Lion by James Daugherty (Viking)—charcoal rubbed off on light gray transfer and rubbed in (?)

1940 / WINNER

Abraham Lincoln by Ingri and Edgar Parin d'Aulaire (Doubleday)—lithographic pencil on stone

HONORS

Cock-a-Doodle-Doo by Berta and Elmer Hader (Macmillan)—watercolor

Madeline by Ludwig Bemelmans (Viking)—brush, pen, and watercolor (?)

The Ageless Story; Illustrated by Lauren Ford (Dodd)—painting; touches of gold leaf (?)

1941 / WINNER

They Were Strong and Good by Robert Lawson (Viking)—brush and ink

HONOR

April's Kittens by Clare Newberry (Harper)—ink, charcoal, and watercolor

1942 / WINNER

Make Way for Ducklings by Robert McCloskey (Viking)— lithographic crayon on stone

HONORS

An American ABC by Maud and Miska Petersham (Macmillan)— pencil and pre-separated watercolor

In My Mother's House by Ann Nolan Clark; Illustrated by Velino Herrera (Viking)—medium not known

Paddle-to-the-Sea by Holling C. Holling (Houghton)—full-color oil paintings

Nothing at All by Wanda Gág (Coward)—original lithographs in color

1943 / WINNER

The Little House by Virginia Lee Burton (Houghton)—watercolor

HONORS

Dash and Dart by Mary and Conrad Buff (Viking)—lithographs (?)

Marshmallow by Clare Newberry (Harper)—charcoal (?)

1944 / WINNER

Many Moons by James Thurber; Illustrated by Louis Slobodkin (HBJ)—pen and ink; watercolor

HONORS

Small Rain: Verses from the Bible; Selected by Jessie Orton Jones; Illustrated by Elizabeth Orton Jones (Viking)—medium not known

Pierre Pigeon by Lee Kingman; Illustrated by Arnold E. Bare (Houghton)—preseparated gouache and ink drawings

The Mighty Hunter by Berta and Elmer Hader (Macmillan)—watercolor

A Child's Good Night Book by Margaret Wise Brown; Illustrated by Jean Charlot (Scott)—crayon drawings

Good-Luck Horse by Chih–Yi Chan; Illustrated by Plato Chan (Whittlesey)—pen and ink; wash (?)

1945 / WINNER

Prayer for a Child by Rachel Field; Illustrated by Elizabeth Orton Jones (Macmillan)— pen and ink; watercolor

HONORS

Mother Goose; Illustrated by Tasha Tudor (Oxford)—graphite and watercolor (?)

In the Forest by Marie Hall Ets (Viking)—paper batik

Yonie Wondernose by Marguerite de Angeli (Doubleday)—color separations done in pen, ink, pencil, and watercolor

The Christmas Anna Angel by Ruth Sawyer; Illustrated by Kate Seredy (Viking)— medium not known

1946 / WINNER

The Rooster Crows by Maud and Miska Petersham (Macmillan)—lithograph pencil with color separations on acetate

HONORS

Little Lost Lamb by Golden MacDonald; Illustrated by Leonard Weisgard (Doubleday)—medium not known

Sing Mother Goose by Opal Wheeler; Illustrated by Marjorie Torrey (Dutton)— medium not known

My Mother Is the Most Beautiful Woman in the World by Becky Reyher; Illustrated by Ruth C. Gannett (Lothrop)—original gouache and watercolor reproduced by four-match process using lithographic crayon

You Can Write Chinese by Kurt Wiese (Viking)—ink and watercolor separations

1947 / WINNER

The Little Island by Golden MacDonald; Illustrated by Leonard Weisgard (Doubleday)—gouache

HONORS

Boats on the River by Marjorie Flack; Illustrated by Jay Hyde Barnum (Viking)—medium not known

Timothy Turtle by Al Graham; Illustrated by Tony Palazzo (Welch)—black-and-white pen and ink (?)

Pedro, the Angel of Olvera Street by Leo Politi (Scribner)—medium not known

Sing in Praise: A Collection of Best Loved Hymns by Opal Wheeler; Illustrated by Marjorie Torrey (Dutton)—medium not known

Rain Drop Splash by Alvin Tresselt; Illustrated by Leonard Weisgard (Lothrop)—three colors preseparated with india ink on acetate overlays

1948 / WINNER

White Snow, Bright Snow by Alvin Tresselt; Illustrated by Roger Duvoisin (Lothrop)—acetate separations in india ink

HONORS

Stone Soup by Marcia Brown (Scribner)—ink and watercolor (?)

McElligot's Pool by Dr. Seuss (Random)—pencil and watercolor

Bambino the Clown by Georges Schreiber (Viking)—medium not known

Roger and the Fox by Lavinia Davis; Illustrated by Hildegard Woodward (Doubleday)—ink (?)

Song of Robin Hood; Edited by Anne Malcolmson; Illustrated by Virginia Lee Burton (Houghton)—scratchboard

1949 / WINNER

The Big Snow by Berta and Elmer Hader (Macmillan)—watercolor

HONORS

Blueberries for Sal by Robert McCloskey (Viking)—lithographs (?)

All around the Town by Phyllis McGinley; Illustrated by Helen Stone (Lippincott)—medium not known

Juanita by Leo Politi (Scribner)—tempera (?)

Fish in the Air by Kurt Wiese (Viking)—ink and watercolor

1950 / WINNER

Song of the Swallows by Leo Politi (Scribner)—tempera

HONORS

America's Ethan Allen by Stewart Holbrook; Illustrated by Lynd Ward (Houghton)—full-color gouache paintings

The Wild Birthday Cake by Lavinia Davis; Illustrated by Hildegard Woodward (Doubleday)—medium not known

The Happy Day by Ruth Krauss; Illustrated by Marc Simont (Harper)—medium not known

Bartholomew and the Oobleck by Dr. Seuss (Random)—pencil, crayon, and watercolor

Henry Fisherman by Marcia Brown (Scribner)—collage (?)

1951 / WINNER

The Egg Tree by Katherine Milhous (Scribner)—tempera

HONORS

Dick Whittington and His Cat by Marcia Brown (Scribner)—linoleum cuts

The Two Reds by Will Lipkind; Illustrated by Nicolas Mordvinoff (HBJ)—acetate separations using pen, ink, and brush

If I Ran the Zoo by Dr. Seuss (Random)—pencil, ink, and watercolor

The Most Wonderful Doll in the World by Phyllis McGinley; Illustrated by Helen Stone (Lippincott)—medium not known

T-Bone, the Baby Sitter by Clare Newberry (Harper)—pen, ink, and charcoal (?)

1952 / WINNER

Finders Keepers by Will Lipkind; Illustrated by Nicolas Mordvinoff (HBJ)—acetate color separations for line reproduction

HONORS

Mr. T. W. Anthony Woo by Marie Hall Ets (Viking)—paper batik

Skipper John's Cook by Marcia Brown (Scribner)—medium not known

All Falling Down by Gene Zion; Illustrated by Margaret Bloy Graham (Harper)—medium not known

Bear Party by William Pène du Bois (Viking)—medium not known

Feather Mountain by Elizabeth Olds (Houghton)—preseparated art and watercolor wash (four-color)

1953 / WINNER

The Biggest Bear by Lynd Ward (Houghton)—opaque watercolor

HONORS

Puss in Boots by Charles Perrault; Illustrated and translated by Marcia Brown (Scribner)—woodcut and watercolor (?)

One Morning in Maine by Robert McCloskey (Viking)—lithographs (?)

Ape in a Cape by Fritz Eichenberg (HBJ)—woodcuts; acetate separations

The Storm Book by Charlotte Zolotow; Illustrated by Margaret Bloy Graham (Harper)—medium not known

Five Little Monkeys by Juliet Kepes (Houghton)—preseparated ink and watercolor wash (four-color)

1954 / WINNER

Madeline's Rescue by Ludwig Bemelmans (Viking)—brush, pen, and watercolor

HONORS

Journey Cake, Ho! by Ruth Sawyer; Illustrated by Robert McCloskey (Viking)— medium not known

When Will the World Be Mine? by Miriam Schlein; Illustrated by Jean Charlot (Scott)—lithographs (?)

The Steadfast Tin Soldier by Hans Christian Andersen; Illustrated by Marcia Brown (Scribner)—medium not known

A Very Special House by Ruth Krauss; Illustrated by Maurice Sendak (Harper)— medium not known

Green Eyes by A. Birnbaum (Capitol)—medium not known

1955 / WINNER

Cinderella by Charles Perrault; Translated and illustrated by Marcia Brown (Scribner)—gouache, crayon, watercolor, and ink

HONORS

Book of Nursery and Mother Goose Rhymes; Illustrated by Marguerite de Angeli (Doubleday)—Sharp Wolf pencils and watercolor

Wheel on the Chimney by Margaret Wise Brown; Illustrated by Tibor Gergely (Lippincott)—gouache (?)

The Thanksgiving Story by Alice Dalgliesh; Illustrated by Helen Sewell (Scribner)— medium not known

1956 / WINNER

Frog Went A-Courtin'; Retold by John Langstaff; Illustrated by Feodor Rojankovsky (HBJ)—brush, ink, and crayon on acetate separations

HONORS

Play with Me by Marie Hall Ets (Viking)—graphite separations

Crow Boy by Taro Yashima (Viking)—pencil and brush separations

1957 / WINNER

A Tree Is Nice by Janice Udry; Illustrated by Marc Simont (Harper)—gouache over watercolor

HONORS

Mr. Penny's Race Horse by Marie Hall Ets (Viking)—paper batik

1 Is One by Tasha Tudor (Walck)—graphite and watercolor (?)

Anatole by Eve Titus; Illustrated by Paul Galdone (McGraw)—pen and ink with gray wash over graphite with paper collage (?)

Gillespie and the Guards by Benjamin Elkin; Illustrated by James Daugherty (Viking)—charcoal rubbed off on light gray transfer and inked (?)

Lion by William Pène du Bois (Viking)—pen and india ink; color preseparated on Dinobase with lithographic pencil

1958 / WINNER

Time of Wonder by Robert McCloskey (Viking)—casein

HONORS

Fly High, Fly Low by Don Freeman (Viking)—colored pencil accented by outlines in ink

Anatole and the Cat by Eve Titus; Illustrated by Paul Galdone (McGraw)—pen and ink with gray wash over graphite with paper collage (?)

1959 / WINNER

Chanticleer and the Fox; Adapted from Chaucer and illustrated by Barbara Cooney (Crowell)—preseparated art: black and white on scratchboard; colors on Dinobase

HONORS

The House That Jack Built by Antonio Frasconi (HBJ)—woodcuts

What Do You Say, Dear? by Sesyle Joslin; Illustrated by Maurice Sendak (Scott)—pen and ink with watercolor wash separations

Umbrella by Taro Yashima (Viking)—watercolor; pencil and brush for direct separations

1960 / WINNER

Nine Days to Christmas by Marie Hall Ets and Aurora Labastida; Illustrated by Marie Hall Ets (Viking)—pencil on Dinobase

HONORS

Houses from the Sea by Alice E. Goudey; Illustrated by Adrienne Adams (Scribner)—watercolor (?)

The Moon Jumpers by Janice Udry; Illustrated by Maurice Sendak (Harper)—tempera

1961 / WINNER

Baboushka and the Three Kings by Ruth Robbins; Illustrated by Nicolas Sidjakov (Parnassus)—tempera and felt-tip pen in four colors

HONOR

Inch by Inch by Leo Lionni (Obolensky)—rice paper collage and crayon

1962 / WINNER

Once a Mouse by Marcia Brown (Scribner)—woodcuts and watercolor

HONORS

The Fox Went Out on a Chilly Night; Illustrated by Peter Spier (Doubleday)—pen and ink and watercolor on blue boards

Little Bear's Visit by Else Holmelund Minarik; Illustrated by Maurice Sendak (Harper)—pen and ink with wash separations

The Day We Saw the Sun Come Up by Alice E. Goudey; Illustrated by Adrienne Adams (Scribner)—graphite and gray wash with white gouache separations

1963 / WINNER

The Snowy Day by Ezra Jack Keats (Viking)—collage: papers, paints, and gum-eraser stamps

HONORS

The Sun Is a Golden Earring by Natalia M. Belting; Illustrated by Bernarda Bryson (Holt)—pencil

Mr. Rabbit and the Lovely Present by Charlotte Zolotow; Illustrated by Maurice Sendak (Harper)—watercolor

1964 / WINNER

Where the Wild Things Are by Maurice Sendak (Harper)—india ink line over full-color tempera

HONORS

Swimmy by Leo Lionni (Pantheon)—watercolor, rubber stamping, and pencil

All in the Morning Early by Sorche Nic Leodhas; Illustrated by Evaline Ness (Holt)—medium not known

Mother Goose and Nursery Rhymes; Illustrated by Philip Reed (Atheneum)—engravings on wood

1965 / WINNER

May I Bring a Friend? by Beatrice Schenk de Regniers; Illustrated by Beni Montresor (Atheneum)—pen-and-ink drawings on board in black with solid overlays and screened overlays on acetate

HONORS

Rain Makes Applesauce by Julian Scheer; Illustrated by Marvin Bileck (Holiday)—pencil and watercolors (?)

The Wave by Margaret Hodges; Illustrated by Blair Lent (Houghton)—ink and cardboard cutouts

A Pocketful of Cricket by Rebecca Caudill; Illustrated by Evaline Ness (Holt)—medium not known

1966 / WINNER

Always Room for One More by Sorche Nic Leodhas; Illustrated by Nonny Hogrogian (Holt)—three-color preseparated art using pen for black line and pastels and wash for color

HONORS

Hide and Seek Fog by Alvin Tresselt; Illustrated by Roger Duvoisin (Lothrop)—full-color gouache

Just Me by Marie Hall Ets (Viking)—paper batik

Tom Tit Tot by Evaline Ness (Holt)—woodcuts

1967 / WINNER

Sam, Bangs & Moonshine by Evaline Ness (Holt)—three-color preseparated art using Japanese pen and wash; printer's ink; roller; string

HONOR

One Wide River to Cross by Barbara Emberley; Illustrated by Ed Emberley (Prentice)—woodcuts

1968 / WINNER

Drummer Hoff by Barbara Emberley; Illustrated by Ed Emberley (Prentice)—woodcuts and ink

HONORS

Frederick by Leo Lionni (Pantheon)—collage with mixed media

Seashore Story by Yashima (Viking)—watercolor and pastel

The Emperor and the Kite by Jane Yolen; Illustrated by Ed Young (World)—paper cuts

1969 / WINNER

The Fool of the World and the Flying Ship; Retold by Arthur Ransome; Illustrated by Uri Shulevitz (Farrar)—pen and brush with black and colored inks

HONOR

Why the Sun and the Moon Live in the Sky by Elphinstone Dayrell; Illustrated by Blair Lent (Houghton)—preseparated pen and ink in three colors

1970 / WINNER

Sylvester and the Magic Pebble by William Steig (Windmill)—watercolor

HONORS

Goggles! by Ezra Jack Keats (Macmillan)—oil paint and collage

Alexander and the Wind-Up Mouse by Leo Lionni (Pantheon)—collage

Pop Corn and Ma Goodness by Edna Mitchell Preston; Illustrated by Robert Andrew Parker (Viking)—watercolor

Thy Friend, Obadiah by Brinton Turkle (Viking)—medium not known

The Judge by Harve Zemach; Illustrated by Margot Zemach (Farrar)—watercolor, pen and ink

1971 / WINNER

A Story A Story by Gail E. Haley (Atheneum)—woodcuts

HONORS

The Angry Moon by William Sleator; Illustrated by Blair Lent (Atlantic/Little)—pen-and-ink drawings with acrylic glazes; full-color paintings

Frog and Toad Are Friends by Arnold Lobel (Harper)—pencil drawings in three colors

In the Night Kitchen by Maurice Sendak (Harper)—line drawings and wash

1972 / WINNER

One Fine Day by Nonny Hogrogian (Macmillan)—acrylic paintings with turpentine on gesso panels

HONORS

Hildilid's Night by Cheli Duran Ryan; Illustrated by Arnold Lobel (Macmillan)—pen-and-ink drawings with yellow overlays

If All the Seas Were One Sea by Janina Domanska (Macmillan)—etchings on zinc plates with brush-and-ink overlays

Moja Means One by Muriel Feelings; Illustrated by Tom Feelings (Dial)—graphite and paper collage

1973 / WINNER

The Funny Little Woman by Arlene Mosel; Illustrated by Blair Lent (Dutton)—pen-and-ink line drawings with full-color acrylic glazes; full-color paintings

HONORS

Anansi the Spider; Adapted and illustrated by Gerald McDermott (Holt)—artwork preseparated in four colors with outline in ink

Hosie's Alphabet by Hosea, Tobias, and Lisa Baskin; Illustrated by Leonard Baskin (Viking)—watercolor

Snow White and the Seven Dwarfs; Translated by Randall Jarrell; Illustrated by Nancy Ekholm Burkert (Farrar)—brush and colored inks

When Clay Sings by Byrd Baylor; Illustrated by Tom Bahti (Scribner)—medium not known

1974 / WINNER

Duffy and the Devil; Retold by Harve Zemach; Pictures by Margot Zemach (Farrar)—pen-and-ink drawings with watercolor

HONORS

Three Jovial Huntsmen by Susan Jeffers (Bradbury)—pen-and-ink drawings with wash overlays painted in oils

Cathedral by David Macaulay (Houghton)—pen and ink

1975 / WINNER

Arrow to the Sun by Gerald McDermott (Viking)—gouache and ink; black line preseparated

HONOR

Jambo Means Hello by Muriel Feelings; Illustrated by Tom Feelings (Dial)—graphite and paper collage

1976 / WINNER

Why Mosquitoes Buzz in People's Ears by Verna Aardema; Pictures by Leo and Diane Dillon (Dial)—india ink; watercolor; pastels; vellum and frisket masks

HONORS

The Desert Is Theirs by Byrd Baylor; Illustrated by Peter Parnall (Scribner)—pen and ink (?)

Strega Nona; Retold and illustrated by Tomie de Paola (Prentice)—watercolor and felt-tip pen over graphite

1977 / WINNER

Ashanti to Zulu: African Traditions by Margaret Musgrove; Pictures by Leo and Diane Dillon (Dial)—pastels, watercolors, and acrylics

HONORS

The Amazing Bone by William Steig (Farrar)—watercolor (?)

The Contest; Retold and illustrated by Nonny Hogrogian (Greenwillow)—colored pencils and crayons for full color; pencil drawings for black and white

Fish for Supper by M. B. Goffstein (Dial)—ink drawings

The Golem by Beverly Brodsky McDermott (Lippincott)—gouache, watercolor, dye, and ink

Hawk, I'm Your Brother by Byrd Baylor; Illustrated by Peter Parnall (Scribner)—pen and ink (?)

1978 / WINNER

Noah's Ark by Peter Spier (Doubleday)—F pencil on paper; watercolor and white pencil; negatives scratched

HONORS

Castle by David Macaulay (Houghton)—pen and ink

It Could Always Be Worse; Retold and illustrated by Margot Zemach (Farrar)—watercolor (?)

1979 / WINNER

The Girl Who Loved Wild Horses by Paul Goble (Bradbury)—full-color pen and ink and watercolor

HONORS

Freight Train by Donald Crews (Greenwillow)—preseparated art; airbrush with transparent dyes

The Way to Start a Day by Byrd Baylor; Illustrated by Peter Parnall (Scribner)—pen and ink (?)

1980 / WINNER

Ox-Cart Man by Donald Hall; Pictures by Barbara Cooney (Viking) —acrylics on gesso-coated board

HONORS

Ben's Trumpet by Rachel Isadora (Greenwillow)—pen and ink

The Garden of Abdul Gasazi by Chris Van Allsburg (Houghton)—carbon pencil on Strathmore paper

The Treasure by Uri Shulevitz (Farrar)—watercolor with black line on acetate

1981 / WINNER

Fables by Arnold Lobel (Harper)—gouache and pencil

HONORS

The Bremen-Town Musicians; Retold and illustrated by Ilse Plume (Doubleday)—colored pencil and graphite (?)

The Grey Lady and the Strawberry Snatcher by Molly Bang (Four Winds)—watercolor, sometimes with white gouache undercoat on gray construction paper

Mice Twice by Joseph Low (McElderry/Atheneum)—watercolor and pen and ink (?)

Truck by Donald Crews (Greenwillow)—four halftone separations with black line drawings

1982 / WINNER

Jumanji by Chris Van Allsburg (Houghton)—conté pencil with conté dust

HONORS

Where the Buffaloes Begin by Olaf Baker; Drawings by Stephen Gammell (Warne)—pencil drawings (?)

On Market Street by Arnold Lobel; Illustrated by Anita Lobel (Greenwillow)—watercolor and pen and ink

Outside over There by Maurice Sendak (Harper)—medium not known

A Visit to William Blake's Inn by Nancy Willard; Illustrated by Alice and Martin Provensen (HBJ)—medium not known

1983 / WINNER

Shadow by Blaise Cendrars; Translated and illustrated by Marcia Brown (Scribner)—collage: paper, woodcuts, acrylics

HONORS

A Chair for My Mother by Vera Williams (Greenwillow)—watercolor

When I Was Young in the Mountains by Cynthia Rylant; Illustrated by Diane Goode (Dutton)—watercolor and fine-colored pencil

1984 / WINNER

The Glorious Flight: Across the Channel with Louis Blériot by Alice and Martin Provensen (Viking)—acrylic and pen and ink

HONORS

Little Red Riding Hood; Retold and illustrated by Trina Schart Hyman (Holiday House)—ink and acrylic (?)

Ten, Nine, Eight by Molly Bang (Greenwillow)—gouache (poster paint)

1985 / WINNER

Saint George and the Dragon; Retold by Margaret Hodges; Illustrated by Trina
Schart Hyman (Little, Brown)—india ink and acrylic

HONORS

Hansel and Gretel; Retold by Rika Lesser; Illustrated by Paul O. Zelinsky (Dodd)—
oil paintings

Have You Seen My Duckling? by Nancy Tafuri (Greenwillow)—watercolors and
pastels

The Story of Jumping Mouse; Retold and illustrated by John Steptoe (Lothrop)—
graphite pencil and india ink on paper

1986 / WINNER

The Polar Express by Chris Van Allsburg (Houghton)—full-color oil pastel on
pastel paper

HONORS

The Relatives Came by Cynthia Rylant; Illustrated by Stephen Gammell
(Bradbury)— graphite and colored pencil

King Bidgood's in the Bathtub by Audrey Wood; Illustrated by Don Wood (HBJ)—
oil on pressed wood (?)

1987 / WINNER

Hey, Al by Arthur Yorinks; Illustrated by Richard Egielski (Farrar) —watercolor

HONORS

The Village of Round and Square Houses by Ann Grifalconi (Little, Brown)—
pastels (?)

Alphabatics by Suse MacDonald (Bradbury)—cells, vinyl acrylic; gouache

Rumpelstiltskin; Retold and illustrated by Paul O. Zelinsky (Dutton)—oil paintings

1988 / WINNER

Owl Moon by Jane Yolen; Illustrated by John Schoenherr (Philomel)—pen and ink
and watercolor

HONOR

Mufaro's Beautiful Daughters by John Steptoe (Lothrop)—crosshatched pen and
ink and watercolor

1989 / WINNER

Song and Dance Man by Karen Ackerman; Illustrated by Stephen Gammell (Knopf)— line drawings in colored pencil

HONORS

The Boy of the Three-Year Nap by Dianne Snyder; Illustrated by Allen Say (Houghton)— brush-line, pen and ink, and watercolor

Free Fall by David Wiesner (Lothrop)—watercolor

Goldilocks and the Three Bears by James Marshall (Dial)—pen and ink and water-color

Mirandy and Brother Wind by Patricia C. McKissack; Illustrated by Jerry Pinkney (Knopf)—pencil and watercolor

1990 / WINNER

Lon Po Po by Ed Young (Philomel)—watercolor and pastels

HONORS

Bill Peet: An Autobiography by Bill Peet (Houghton)—pencil

Color Zoo by Lois Ehlert (Lippincott)—paper collage and die-cut forms

Hershel and the Hanukkah Goblins by Eric Kimmel; Illustrated by Trina Schart Hyman (Holiday House)—india ink and acrylic paint

The Talking Eggs by Robert San Souci; Illustrated by Jerry Pinkney (Dial)—pencil, colored-pencil, and watercolor

1991 / WINNER

Black and White by David Macaulay (Houghton) "Seeing Things"—watercolor; "Problem Parents"—ink line and wash; "A Waiting Game"—watercolor and gouache; "Udder Confusion"—gouache paint

HONORS

"More, More, More," Said the Baby: 3 Love Stories by Vera B. Williams (Greenwillow)— gouache paints; lettering painted in watercolor based on Gill Sans Extra Bold Print

Puss in Boots by Fred Marcellino (di Capua/Farrar)—colored pencil on taupe textured illustration paper

1992 / WINNER

Tuesday by David Wiesner (Clarion)—watercolor

HONOR

Tar Beach by Faith Ringgold (Crown)—acrylic on canvas

1993 / WINNER

Mirette on the High Wire by Emily Arnold McCully (Putnam)—watercolor

HONORS

Seven Blind Mice by Ed Young (Philomel)—paper collage

The Stinky Cheese Man & Other Fairly Stupid Tales by Jon Scieszka; Illustrated by Lane Smith (Viking)—oil and mixed media

Working Cotton by Sherley Anne Williams; Illustrated by Carole Byard (HBJ)—acrylic on Stonehenge white paper

1994 / WINNER

Grandfather's Journey by Allen Say (Houghton)—watercolor

HONORS

Peppe the Lamplighter by Elisa Bartone; Illustrated by Ted Lewin (Lothrop)—watercolor

In the Small, Small Pond by Denise Fleming (Holt)—colored cotton pulp poured through hand-cut stencils

Owen by Kevin Henkes (Greenwillow)—watercolor paints and black ink

Raven: A Trickster Tale from the Pacific Northwest by Gerald McDermott (Harcourt)—gouache, colored pencil, and pastel on heavyweight, cold-press watercolor paper

Yo! Yes? by Chris Raschka (Orchard)—watercolor and charcoal pencil

1995 / WINNER

Smoky Night by Eve Bunting; Illustrated by David Diaz (Harcourt)—acrylic paintings set against mixed media collage backgrounds

HONORS

Swamp Angel by Anne Isaacs; Illustrated by Paul O. Zelinsky (Dutton)—oil on cherry, maple, and birch veneers

John Henry by Julius Lester; Illustrated by Jerry Pinkney (Dial)—pencil, colored pencil, and watercolor

Time Flies by Eric Rohmann (Crown)—oil

1996 / WINNER

Officer Buckle and Gloria by Peggy Rathmann (Putnam)—watercolor and ink

HONORS

Alphabet City by Stephen T. Johnson (Viking)—pastels, watercolors, gouache, and charcoal on hot pressed watercolor paper

Zin! Zin! Zin! a Violin by Lloyd Moss; Illustrated by Marjorie Priceman (Simon & Schuster)—gouache

The Faithful Friend by Robert D. San Souci; Illustrated by Brian Pinkney (Simon & Schuster)—scratchboard and oil

Tops & Bottoms; Adapted and illustrated by Janet Stevens (Harcourt)—watercolor, colored pencil, and gesso on paper made by hand by Ray Tomasso, Denver, Colorado

1997 / WINNER

Golem by David Wisniewski (Clarion)—color-aid, coral, and bark cut papers

HONORS

Hush! A Thai Lullaby by Minfong Ho; Illustrated by Holly Meade (Orchard)—cut-paper collage with ink

The Graphic Alphabet by David Pelletier (Orchard)—computer-generated images reproduced in full color

The Paperboy by Dav Pilkey (Orchard)—acrylics and india ink

Starry Messenger by Peter Sís (Farrar Straus Giroux)—pen and brown ink and watercolor

1998 / WINNER

Rapunzel by Paul O. Zelinsky (Dutton)—oil reproduced in full color

HONORS

The Gardener by Sarah Stewart; Illustrated by David Small (Farrar)—watercolor, ink pen line, and crayon

Harlem by Walter Dean Myers; Illustrated by Christopher Myers (Scholastic)—ink, gouache, and cut-paper collage

There Was an Old Lady Who Swallowed a Fly by Simms Taback (Viking)—mixed media and collage on kraft paper in color

1999 / WINNER

Snowflake Bentley by Jacqueline Briggs Martin; Illustrated by Mary Azarian (Houghton)—woodcuts, hand-tinted with watercolors

HONORS

Duke Ellington by Andrea Davis Pinkney; Illustrated by Brian Pinkney (Hyperion)— scratchboard renderings with gouache, luma dyes, and oil paint

No, David! by David Shannon (Blue Sky/Scholastic)—acrylics and colored pencil

Snow by Uri Shulevitz (Farrar Straus Giroux)—ink and watercolor washes

Tibet: Through the Red Box by Peter Sís (Farrar Straus Giroux)—watercolor, pen and ink, and oil pastel

2000 / WINNER

Joseph Had a Little Overcoat by Simms Taback (Viking)—watercolor, gouache, pencil, ink, and collage

HONORS

A Child's Calendar by John Updike; Illustrated by Trina Schart Hyman (Holiday House)—pen and ink and watercolor

Sector 7 by David Wiesner (Clarion)—watercolor

When Sofie Gets Angry—Really, Really Angry by Molly Bang (Scholastic)—gouache

The Ugly Duckling; Adapted and illustrated by Jerry Pinkney (Morrow)—watercolor

2001 / WINNER

So You Want to Be President? by Judith St. George; Illustrated by David Small (Philomel)—watercolor, ink, and pastel chalk

HONORS

Casey at the Bat: A Ballad of the Republic Sung in the Year 1888 by Ernest Lawrence Thayer; Illustrated by Christopher Bing (Handprint)—pen and ink scratchboard engravings

Click, Clack, Moo: Cows That Type by Doreen Cronin; Illustrated by Betsy Lewin (Simon & Schuster)—watercolor

Olivia by Ian Falconer (Atheneum)—charcoal and gouache

2002 / WINNER

The Three Pigs by David Wiesner (Clarion)—watercolor, gouache, colored inks, pencil, and colored pencil on Fabriano hot press paper

HONORS

The Stray Dog by Marc Simont (HarperCollins)—watercolor, gouache

Martin's Big Words: The Life of Dr. Martin Luther King, Jr. by Doreen Rappaport; Illustrated by Bryan Collier (Hyperion Books for Children/Jump at the Sun)—watercolor, cut-paper collage

The Dinosaurs of Waterhouse Hawkins: An Illuminating History of Mr. Waterhouse Hawkins, Artist and Lecturer by Barbara Kerley; Illustrated by Brian Selznick (Scholastic Press)—acrylics

2003 / WINNER

My Friend Rabbit by Eric Rohmann (Millbrook)—hand-colored relief prints (watercolors)

HONORS

The Spider and the Fly by Mary Howitt; Illustrated by Tony DiTerlizzi (Simon & Schuster)—lamp black and titanium white holbein Acryla gouache and Berol Prismacolor pencil on Strathmore 5-ply, plate Bristol board and reproduced in silver and black duotone, graphite, and Adobe Photoshop

Hondo & Fabian by Peter McCarty (Holt)—pencil on watercolor paper

Noah's Ark by Jerry Pinkney (North-South)—pencil, colored pencil, watercolors

2004 / WINNER

The Man Who Walked between the Towers by Mordicai Gerstein (Roaring Brook Press, a division of Millbrook)—pen and ink and oil paint on paper

HONORS

Ella Sarah Gets Dressed by Margaret Chodos-Irvine (Harcourt)—various print-making techniques on Rives paper

What Do You Do with a Tail like This? by Steve Jenkins and Robin Page (Houghton)—cut-paper collage

Don't Let the Pigeon Drive the Bus by Mo Willems (Hyperion)—Calligraphic cartoon drawings in dark marking pencil; scanned, cleaned, and colored in Photoshop

SOME USEFUL DEFINITIONS

Acetate—a clear, plastic film used for overlays.

Airbrush—a mechanical painting tool that emits a fine spray of liquid or ink.

Batik—a wax-resistant process in which the design or image is first painted on the surface in wax so that, when the surface is dyed, the wax sections will not take the color.

Binder—the ingredient of a paint that holds together the particles of pigment and fixes them into a continuous film as the paint dries.

Color preseparation—the process by which an artist prepares, manually, the art to be printed in a four-, three-, or two-color book. This is done by preparing a master preseparation and overlays, each specifying a color to be reproduced for the image(s) contained in the area of the picture. When all of the overlays are printed together, the colors form the final picture.

Conté pencil—square-sectioned drawing chalks in black, white, sanguine, and sepia.

Dinobase—acetate sand-blasted to roughen the surface, making it similar to a lithographic stone; no longer used.

Dye—a coloring agent soluble in liquid that imparts color to a surface by being absorbed.

Engraving—any process by which a linear design is made on the surface of a hard and durable substance.

F pencil—a medium-hard graphite pencil.

Four-color process—a printing process in which the full range of the colors of an image is reproduced by means of four separate printing plates (black, blue, red, and yellow), which can be separated via camera, computer, or artist. After the separations, the plates are printed one on top of another in transparent process inks, as dictated by the separations, to create the final picture.

Frisket mask—a thin paper placed over an area not to be colored during painting or airbrushing.

Gouache—a method of painting with opaque colors.

Graphite—a carbon in stick form used for drawing.

India ink—a permanent black ink made of lampblack and glue binder.

Linoleum cuts—a relief printing process in which the image or design is cut into the surface of a block of linoleum.

Lithograph—a print made by drawing on limestone or a zinc plate with a greasy material, then wetting the plate and applying greasy ink that will only adhere to the drawn line. Dampened paper is then rubbed over the stone with a special press to create the final print. A lithographic crayon or pencil is often used for drawing on the lithographic stone, which is a block of limestone with its surface ground so an image can be made upon it. In offset lithography, the image is first transferred to an intermediate surface (a rubber blanket) before it is transferred to the paper.

Overlay—a transparent or translucent film attached to artwork carrying additional detail to be reproduced.

Paint—a substance consisting of a pigment evenly dispersed in a liquid which, when applied to a surface as a fluid, dries into a continuous film of color. In acrylic paint, the pigment is dispersed in an emulsion binder that is a liquid form of acrylic resin. In oil paint, the pigment is dispersed in a drying oil (usually linseed). In watercolor, the finely ground pigment is dispersed in a water-soluble gum binder and is transparent; gouache is a watercolor that uses opaque rather than transparent colors; tempera is an opaque watercolor paint in which the pigment is ground in water and mixed with egg yolk; it can also be poster paint.

Pastels—a drawing medium consisting of pigment mixed with gum binder, rolled or compressed into stick form.

Pigment—a finely ground colored powder that may be mixed with a liquid vehicle to make paint.

Scratchboard—an ink technique in which a white board is covered with india ink and a design or image is scratched into it.

Wash—an application of ink or watercolor heavily diluted with water to form a thin film of transparent color.

Woodcut—a relief printing process in which the image or design is cut into the surface of a plank-grain wood block.

BIBLIOGRAPHY

Children's Books: 1955–1957. New York: American Institute of Graphic Arts, 1958.

Children's Books: 1958–1960. New York: American Institute of Graphic Arts, 1960.

Children's Books: 1961–1962. New York: American Institute of Graphic Arts, 1962.

Cianciolo, Patricia J., ed. *Picture Books for Children.* 4th ed. American Library Assn., 1997.

de Angeli, Marguerite. *Butter at the Old Price.* Garden City: Doubleday, 1971.

Illustrations for Children: The Gladys English Collection. Sacramento: California Library Assn., Gladys English Memorial Collection Committee, 1963.

Jones, Helen. *Robert Lawson, Illustrator.* Boston: Little, 1972.

Kingman, Lee, and others. *Illustrators of Children's Books, 1957–1966.* Boston: Horn Book, 1968.

Kingman, Lee, ed. *Newbery and Caldecott Medal Books: 1956–1965.* Boston: Horn Book, 1965.

Kingman, Lee, ed. *Newbery and Caldecott Medal Books: 1966–1975.* Boston: Horn Book, 1975.

Kingman, Lee, ed. *Newbery and Caldecott Medal Books: 1976–1985.* Boston: Horn Book, 1986.

Lanes, Selma G. *The Art of Maurice Sendak.* New York: Abrams, 1980.

Larkin, David, ed. *The Art of Nancy Ekholm Burkert.* New York: Harper, 1977.

Lucie-Smith, Edward. *The Thames and Hudson Dictionary of Art Terms.* London: Thames & Hudson, 1984.

Martin, Judy. *The Longman Dictionary of Art.* Harlow, Eng.: Longman Group, 1986.

Miller, Bertha Mahony, and others. *Caldecott Medal Books: 1938–1957.* Boston: Horn Book, 1957.

Quick, John. *Artists' and Illustrators' Encyclopedia,* II ed. New York: McGraw-Hill, 1977.

Shulevitz, Uri. *Writing with Pictures.* New York: Watson-Guptill, 1985.

Viguers, Ruth Hill, and others. *Illustrators of Children's Books, 1946–1956.* Boston: Horn Book, 1958.

Also consulted: all issues of *Horn Book Magazine:* 1938–1986.

AUTHOR/ILLUSTRATOR INDEX

Aardema, Verna, 109
Ackerman, Karen, 101
Adams, Adrienne, 118, 120
Adams, Julia Davis, 78, 79
Alexander, Lloyd, 45, 48
Alger, Leclaire (as Sorche Nic Leodhas),
    49, 116, 117
Allee, Marjorie, 77
Andersen, Hans Christian, 124
Angelo, Valenti, 70, 71
Armer, Laura Adams, 76, 136
Armer, Sidney, 76
Armstrong, William, 44
Artzybasheff, Boris, 68, 82, 137
Atwater, Florence, 70
Atwater, Richard, 70
Avi, 22, 30
Azarian, Mary, 93

Babbitt, Natalie, 44
Bahti, Tom, 111
Bailey, Carolyn Sherwin, 63
Baity, Elizabeth, 58
Baker, Olaf, 105
Bang, Molly, 93, 104, 106
Bannon, Laura, 71
Bare, Arnold E., 134
Barkley, James, 44
Barnes, Nancy, 63
Barney, Maginel Wright, 82
Barnum, Jay Hyde, 130
Bartone, Elisa, 97
Baskin, Hosea, 111
Baskin, Leonard, 111
Baskin, Lisa, 111
Baskin, Tobias, 111

Bauer, Joan, 23
Bauer, Marion Dane, 33
Baylor, Byrd, 108, 109, 110, 111
Beddows, Eric, 31
Belting, Natalia M., 118
Bemelmans, Ludwig, 72, 123, 136
Bennett, John, 81
Bernstein, Zena, 42
Berry, Erick, pseud. (Allena Best), 74, 75,
    78
Best, Allena (as Erick Berry), 74, 75, 78
Best, Herbert, 78
Besterman, Catherine, 62
Bianco, Margery, 72
Bileck, Marvin, 117
Bing, Christopher, 91
Birch, Reginald, 84
Birnbaum, A., 124
Bishop, Claire Huchet, 56, 62
Bjorklund, Lorence, 57
Blair, Helen, 64
Blegvad, Erik, 37, 52
Bloom, Lloyd, 34
Blos, Joan, 38
Blumberg, Rhoda, 33
Bock, Vera, 80
Bond, Nancy, 39
Bontemps, Arna, 61
Bowen, William, 84
Bowman, James Cloyd, 71
Boyle, Mildred, 66, 68, 69, 71
Brink, Carol Ryrie, 73
Brittain, Bill, 35
Brooks, Bruce, 29, 34
Brown, Marcia, 104, 118, 123, 124, 125,
    126, 127, 128, 129

Brown, Margaret Wise, 123
Brown, Margaret Wise (as Golden
    MacDonald), 130, 131, 133
Bryant, Samuel, 47
Bryson, Bernarda, 118
Buff, Conrad, 57, 59, 63, 134
Buff, Mary, 57, 59, 63, 134
Bunting, Eve, 96
Burger, Carl, 54
Burglon, Nora, 76
Burkert, Nancy Ekholm, 111
Burton, Virginia Lee, 130, 134
Byard, Carole, 99
Byars, Betsy, 44

Carlson, Natalie S., 52
Carr, Mary Jane, 68
Caudill, Rebecca, 60, 116
Cendrars, Blaise, 104
Chan, Chih-Yi, 133
Chan, Plato, 133
Chapman, Frederick, 64
Chappell, Warren, 62
Charlot, Jean, 55, 56, 57, 124, 133
Chastain, Madye Lee, 63
Chaucer, Geoffrey, 120
Chodos-Irvine, Margaret, 89
Chrisman, Arthur Bowie, 82
Clark, Ann Nolan, 57, 135
Cleary, Beverly, 34, 37, 39
Coatsworth, Elizabeth, 78
Cober, Alan, 41
Coblentz, Catherine, 61
CoConis, Ted, 44
Collier, Bryan, 91
Collier, Christopher, 40
Collier, James Lincoln, 40
Colum, Padraic, 74, 83, 84
Coman, Carolyn, 27
Conly, Jane Leslie, 28
Coolidge, Olivia, 49
Cooney, Barbara, 61, 107, 120
Cooper, Susan, 40, 41
Cosgrove, John O'Hara, 55
Couloumbis, Audrey, 24
Courlander, Harold, 63

Crawford, Phyllis, 70
Creech, Sharon, 24, 28
Crews, Donald, 106, 107
Cronin, Doreen, 92
Cuffari, Richard, 41
Curtis, Christopher Paul, 24, 27
Cushman, Karen, 27, 28

Dalgliesh, Alice, 56, 57, 65, 123
Daugherty, James, 60, 69, 76, 121, 137
d'Aulaire, Edgar Parin, 76, 136
d'Aulaire, Ingri, 136
Davis, Lavinia, 128, 130
Davis, Mary Gould, 77
Dayrell, Elphinstone, 114
de Angeli, Marguerite, 54, 60, 78, 123, 132
de Gorgoza, Maitland, 77
DeJong, Meindert, 52, 54, 56, 57
de Miskey, Julian, 52
Dennis, Wesley, 61, 63, 64
de Paola, Tomie, 25, 110
de Regniers, Beatrice Schenk, 116
Diamond, Donna, 38
Diaz, David, 96
DiCamillo, Kate, 20, 24
Dillon, Diane, 40, 108, 109
Dillon, Leo, 40, 108, 109
DiTerlizzi, Tony, 90
Dobias, Frank, 75, 81
Domanska, Janina, 112
du Bois, William Pène, 62, 121, 126
Duvoisin, Roger, 65, 116, 129

Eaton, Jeanette, 59, 65, 70, 80
Eckert, Allan, 43
Edmonds, Walter, 67
Egielski, Richard, 102
Ehlert, Lois, 100
Eichenberg, Fritz, 67, 125
Elkin, Benjamin, 121
Emberley, Barbara, 115
Emberley, Ed, 115
Engdahl, Sylvia Louise, 44
Enright, Elizabeth, 53, 70
Estes, Eleanor, 58, 66, 67
Ets, Marie Hall, 116, 119, 122, 126, 132

Falconer, Ian, 92
Falls, C. B., 58, 65
Farmer, Nancy, 22, 26, 28
Feelings, Muriel, 110, 112
Feelings, Tom, 45, 110, 112
Fenner, Carol, 27
Field, Rachel, 77, 79, 132
Finger, Charles, 83
Fischer, Anton Otto, 83
Fish, Helen Dean, 137, 138
Fisher, Cyrus, pseud. (Darwin L. Teilhet), 64
Fisher, Leonard Everett, 51, 52
Flack, Marjorie, 130
Fleischman, Paul, 31, 36
Fleischman, Sid, 32
Fleming, Denise, 97
Floethe, Richard, 61, 64
Forbes, Esther, 66
Ford, Lauren, 136
Foster, Genevieve, 58, 61, 66, 67
Fox, Paula, 34, 41
Frankenberg, Robert, 60
Frasconi, Antonio, 120
Freedman, Russell, 29, 30, 32
Freeman, Don, 121
Fritz, Jean, 36

Gág, Wanda, 75, 81, 135, 137
Gaggin, Eva Roe, 68
Galdone, Paul, 53, 58, 121, 122
Gammell, Stephen, 101, 103, 105
Gannett, Ruth Chrisman, 62, 63, 132
Gannett, Ruth S., 62
Gantos, Jack, 24
Garraty, Gail, 43
Gates, Doris, 68
Gay, Zhenya, 72
Geisel, Theodor Seuss (as Dr. Seuss), 127, 128, 130
George, Jean Craighead, 42, 51
Gergely, Tibor, 123
Gerstein, Mordicai, 88
Giff, Patricia Reilly, 22, 26
Gipson, Fred, 54
Glanzman, Louis, 48

Glass, Andrew, 35, 36
Goble, Paul, 107
Goble, Warwick, 81
Goffstein, M. B., 109
Goode, Diane, 105
Goudey, Alice, 118, 120
Graham, Al, 131
Graham, Margaret Bloy, 125, 126
Gray, Elizabeth Janet, 67, 70, 73, 78
Greene, Bette, 41
Grifalconi, Ann, 47, 102
Gurko, Leo, 53

Hader, Berta, 128, 133, 136
Hader, Elmer, 68, 128, 133, 136
Haley, Gail, 112
Hall, Anna Gertrude, 68
Hall, Donald, 107
Hallock, Grace, 81
Hamilton, Virginia, 31, 36, 40, 43
Handforth, Thomas, 136
Hasselriis, Else, 82
Havighurst, Marion, 61
Havighurst, Walter, 61
Hawes, Charles, 83, 85
Hendrickson, David, 75
Henkes, Kevin, 21, 98
Henry, Marguerite, 61, 63, 64
Herrera, Velino, 135
Heslop, Michael, 40
Hesse, Karen, 25
Hewes, Agnes, 72, 75, 78
Hiasen, Carl, 22
Highwater, Jamake, 39
Ho, Minfong, 95
Hodges, Margaret, 103, 117
Hogrogian, Nonny, 46, 109, 112, 116
Holberg, Richard, 68
Holbrook, Stewart, 128
Holland, Janice, 61
Holling, Holling C., 59, 62, 135
Holm, Jennifer, 25
Honore, Charles, 83
Horvath, Polly, 23
Houser, Lowell, 79
Howitt, Mary, 90

Hubbard, Ralph, 78
Hunt, Irene, 47, 48
Hunt, Mabel Leigh, 60, 67
Hyman, Trina Schart, 92, 100, 103, 104

Isaacs, Anne, 96
Isadora, Rachel, 107
Ish-Kishor, Sulamith, 45
Ishmael, Woodi, 65

Jackson, Richard, 98
James, M. R., 124
James, Will, 82
Jarrell, Randall, 48, 111
Jeffers, Susan, 111
Jenkins, Steve, 89
Jewett, Eleanore, 64
Johansen, Margaret, 79
Johnson, Gerald W., 51, 52
Johnson, Milton, 46, 49
Johnson, Steven T., 95
Jones, Elizabeth Orton, 132, 134
Jones, Idwal, 72
Jones, Jessie Orton, 134
Jones, Wildred, 83
Joslin, Sesyle, 120
Judson, Clara Ingram, 54, 57, 60
Jukes, Mavis, 34

Kalashnikoff, Nicholas, 59
Kalnay, Francis, 52
Karasz, Ilonka, 64
Katchamakoff, Atanas, 73
Keats, Ezra Jack, 113, 118
Keith, Eros, 41
Keith, Harold, 53
Kelly, Eric P., 80
Kendall, Carol, 52
Kepes, Juliet, 125
Kerley, Barbara, 91
Kherdian, David, 38
Kimmel, Eric, 100
Kingman, Lee, 134
Knight, Christopher G., 35
Konigsburg, E. L., 26, 46
Krauss, Ruth, 124, 128

Kredel, Fritz, 53
Krumgold, Joseph, 51, 56
Krush, Beth, 53, 54
Krush, Joe, 53, 54
Kyle, Anne, 75

Labastida, Aurora, 119
Langstaff, John, 122
Langton, Jane, 37
Laning, Edward, 70
Lantz, Paul, 67, 68
Lasky, Kathryn, 35
Latham, Jean Lee, 55
Lathrop, Dorothy P., 75, 77, 79, 137
Lauber, Patricia, 33
Lawson, Robert, 53, 65, 67, 70, 135, 137, 138
Leaf, Munro, 137
LeGuin, Ursula K., 43
L'Engle, Madeleine, 37, 49
Lenski, Lois, 64, 68, 72
Lent, Blair, 111, 113, 114, 117
Leodhas, Sorche Nic, pseud. (Leclaire
    Alger), 49, 116, 117
Lesser, Rika, 103
Lester, Julius, 45, 97
Levine, Gail Carson, 25
Lewin, Betsy, 92
Lewin, Ted, 97
Lewis, Allen, 77
Lewis, Elizabeth, 76
Lide, Alice, 79
Lilly, Charles, 41
Lindquist, Jennie, 55
Lionni, Leo, 113, 115, 117, 119
Lipkind, William (as Will), 125, 127
Lisle, Janet Taylor, 31
Lobel, Anita, 105
Lobel, Arnold, 42, 105, 106, 112, 113
Lofting, Hugh, 84
Lorraine, Walter, 97
Louden, Claire, 59
Louden, George, 59
Low, Joseph, 106
Lownsbery, Eloise, 77
Lowry, Lois, 28, 31
Lufkin, Raymond, 61, 79

Macaulay, David, 99, 108, 111
MacDonald, Golden, pseud. (Margaret Wise Brown), 130, 131, 133. *See also* Brown, Margaret Wise
MacDonald, James, 72, 74
MacDonald, Suse, 102
MacLachlan, Patricia, 33
Malcolmson, Anne, 130
Malkus, Alida, 79
Marcellino, Fred, 100
Marshall, Bernard, 85
Marshall, James, 101
Martin, Anne M., 22
Martin, Jacqueline Briggs, 93
Mathis, Sharon Bell, 40
Maxwell, William, 64
Mazer, Norma Fox, 32
McCarty, Peter, 90
McCloskey, Robert, 121, 124, 125, 129, 134
McCully, Emily Arnold, 98
McDermott, Beverly Brodsky, 109
McDermott, Gerald, 98, 110, 112
McGinley, Phyllis, 127, 129
McGraw, Eloise Jarvis, 26, 50, 58
McKinley, Robin, 34, 36
McKissack, Patricia C., 29, 101
McNeely, Marian Hurd, 80
Meade, Holly, 95
Meader, Stephen, 69
Means, Florence Crannell, 64
Meigs, Cornelia, 74, 76, 81, 85
Miles, Miska, 43
Milhous, Katherine, 65, 126
Miller, Elizabeth, 80
Minarik, Else H., 118
Montgomery, Rutherford, 61
Montresor, Beni, 50, 116
Moon, Carl, 81
Moon, Grace, 81
Moore, Annie Carroll, 83
Moore, Janet Gaylord, 45
Mordvinoff, Nicolas (as Nicolas), 125, 127
Morse, Dorothy B., 60
Mosel, Arlene, 111
Moser, Barry, 31
Moss, Lloyd, 96

Mukerji, Dhan Gopal, 82
Murphy, Jim, 21, 27
Musgrove, Margaret, 108
Myers, Christopher, 94
Myers, Walter Dean, 29, 32, 94

Nadejen, Theodore, 78
Naylor, Phyllis Reynolds, 30
Negri, Rocco, 45
Nelson, Marilyn, 23
Ness, Evaline, 49, 115, 116, 117
Neville, Emily, 49
Newberry, Clare Turlay, 127, 134, 135, 137
Nicolas, pseud. (Nicolas Mordvinoff), 125, 127
North, Sterling, 49

O'Brien, Robert C., 42
O'Dell, Scott, 44, 46, 47, 50
Olds, Elizabeth, 126
Orr, Forrest W., 76
Ostman, Lempi, 79

Page, Robin, 89
Palazzo, Tony, 131
Park, Linda Sue, 23
Parker, Robert Andrew, 114
Parnall, Peter, 43, 108, 109, 110
Parrish, Anne, 60, 79, 83
Paterson, Katherine, 37, 38
Paulsen, Gary, 31, 32, 33
Peck, Richard, 23, 25
Peet, Bill, 100
Pelletier, David, 95
Perrault, Charles, 123, 125
Petersham, Maud, 80, 131, 135
Petersham, Miska, 80, 131, 135
Pilkey, Dav, 95
Pinkney, Andrea Davis, 93
Pinkney, Brian, 93, 96
Pinkney, Jerry, 90, 93, 97, 101
Plume, Ilse, 106
Pogany, Willy, 84
Politi, Leo, 127, 129, 131
Pope, Elizabeth Marie, 41
Porter, Neal, 95

Preston, Edna Mitchell, 114
Price, Christine, 49
Priceman, Marjorie, 96
Provensen, Alice, 36, 104, 106
Provensen, Martin, 36, 104, 106
Pruszynska, Angela, 80

Raible, Alton, 42, 43, 47
Rankin, Louise, 62
Ransome, Arthur, 114
Rappaport, Doreen, 91
Raschka, Chris, 98
Raskin, Ellen, 38, 41
Rathmann, Peggy, 95
Ravielli, Anthony, 55
Rawlings, Marjorie Kinnan, 55
Ray, Ralph, 59
Reed, Philip, 117
Reiss, Johanna, 42
Reyher, Becky, 132
Rhoads, Dorothy, 55
Ringgold, Faith, 99
Robbins, Ruth, 119
Robinson, Mabel, 69, 71
Rohmann, Eric, 90, 97
Rojankovsky, Feodor, 56, 122
Rose, Jack Manley, 70
Rourke, Constance, 72, 74
Ryan, Cheli Duran, 112
Rylant, Cynthia, 29, 33, 103, 105

Sachar, Louis, 25
San Souci, Robert D., 96, 101
Sandoz, Mari, 53
Sauer, Julia, 59, 66
Sawyer, Ruth, 71, 124, 133
Say, Allen, 97, 101
Schaefer, Jack, 51
Scheer, Julian, 117
Schlein, Miriam, 124
Schmidt, Sarah, 75
Schoenherr, John, 42, 43, 49, 102
Scholder, Fritz, 39
Schreiber, Georges, 59, 62, 130
Scieszka, Jon, 98
Seeger, Elizabeth, 74

Selden, George, pseud. (George
    Thompson), 51
Selznick, Brian, 91
Sendak, Maurice, 47, 48, 52, 54, 56, 57,
    105, 113, 117, 118, 120, 124
Seredy, Kate, 63, 69, 71, 73, 133
Seuss, Dr., pseud. (Theodor Seuss Geisel),
    127, 128, 130
Sewell, Helen, 57, 66, 68, 69, 71, 123
Shackell, Rodney, 44
Shannon, David, 93
Shannon, Monica, 73
Sheldon, Myrtle, 77
Shenton, Edward, 69
Shimin, Symeon, 51
Shippen, Katherine, 55, 65
Shulevitz, Uri, 93, 107, 114
Sidjakov, Nicolas, 119
Siegal, Aranka, 37
Siegel, William, 80
Simont, Marc, 91, 121, 128
Singer, Isaac Bashevis, 46, 47
Singmaster, Elsie, 75
Sís, Peter, 32, 94, 95
Sleator, William, 113
Slobodkin, Louis, 66, 67, 133
Small, David, 91, 94
Smith, Alvin, 48
Smith, Lane, 98
Snedeker, Caroline, 75, 82
Snyder, Diane, 101
Snyder, Zilpha Keatley, 42, 43, 47
Sorensen, Virginia, 54
Speare, Elizabeth George, 35, 50, 52
Sperry, Armstrong, 68, 72, 73
Spier, Peter, 108, 119
Spinelli, Jerry, 26, 30
St. George, Judith, 91
Staples, Suzanne Fisher, 31
Steele, Mary Q., 45
Steele, William, 53
Steig, William, 36, 39, 109, 113
Steptoe, John, 102, 103
Stevens, Janet, 96
Stewart, Sarah, 94
Stolz, Mary, 48, 50

Stone, Helen, 127, 129
Stong, Phil, 73
Swift, Hildegarde, 76, 80

Taback, Simms, 92, 94
Tafuri, Nancy, 104
Taylor, Mildred D., 39
Teilhet, Darwin L. (as Cyrus Fisher), 64
Thayer, Ernest Lawrence, 91
Thompson, George (as George Selden), 51
Thurber, James, 133
Tiegreen, Alan, 37, 39
Tietjens, Eunice, 77
Titus, Eve, 121, 122
Todd, Robert, 54
Tolan, Stephanie S., 22
Tomes, Margot, 36
Torrey, Marjorie, 131, 132
Treffinger, Carolyn, 63
Tresselt, Alvin, 116, 129, 131
Trevino, Elizabeth Borton de, 48
Tudor, Tasha, 122, 133
Tunis, Edwin, 50
Turkle, Brinton, 114
Turner, Megan Whalen, 26

Udry, Janice May, 120, 121
Ullman, James, 56
Unwin, Nora S., 59, 67
Updike, John, 92

Van Allsburg, Chris, 103, 105, 107
Van Everen, Jay, 77, 83
van Loon, Hendrik Willem, 84
Van Stockum, Hilda, 74
Varian, George, 85
Voigt, Cynthia, 35
von Schmidt, Harold, 78

Ward, Lynd, 66, 69, 71, 78, 80, 124, 128
Watkins, Bernard, 74
Weik, Mary Hays, 47
Weil, Ann, 58

Weisgard, Leonard, 55, 56, 130, 131
Weiss, Emil, 49
West, Harold, 51
Weston, Christine, 65
Wheeler, Opal, 131, 132
White, E. B., 58
White, Ruth, 27
Whitney, Elinor, 81
Whitney, George Gillett, 70
Wier, Ester, 49
Wiese, Kurt, 62, 63, 73, 76, 129, 132
Wiesner, David, 90, 92, 99, 101
Wilder, Laura Ingalls, 66, 68, 69, 71
Will, pseud. (William Lipkind), 125, 127
Willard, Nancy, 36, 106
Willems, Mo, 89
Williams, Garth, 51, 52, 55, 58
Williams, Sherley Anne, 99
Williams, Vera B., 100, 105
Wisniewski, David, 94
Wojciechowska, Maia, 48
Wolcott, Elizabeth Tyler, 77
Wood, Audrey, 103
Wood, Don, 103
Wood, Harrie, 81
Woodward, Hildegard, 128, 130
Wyeth, N. C., 75

Yashima, Taro, 115, 120, 122
Yates, Elizabeth, 59, 67
Yeats, Jack, 74
Yep, Laurence, 29, 40
Yolen, Jane, 102, 115
Yorinks, Arthur, 102
Young, Ed, 99, 100, 115
Young, Ella, 80, 82

Zelinsky, Paul O., 34, 94, 96, 102, 103
Zemach, Harve, 110, 114
Zemach, Margot, 46, 108, 110, 114
Zion, Gene, 126
Zolotow, Charlotte, 118, 125

TITLE INDEX

The ABC Bunny, 75
Abel's Island, 39
Abraham Lincoln, 136
Abraham Lincoln, Friend of the People, 60
Abraham Lincoln's World, 66
Across Five Aprils, 48
Adam of the Road, 67
After the Rain, 32
Afternoon of the Elves, 31
The Ageless Story, 136
Alexander and the Wind-Up Mouse, 113
All Alone, 56
All Around the Town, 129
All Falling Down, 126
All in the Morning Early, 117
All Sail Set, 73
Along Came a Dog, 52
Alphabatics, 102
Alphabet City, 95
Always Room for One More, 116
The Amazing Bone, 109
America Is Born, 52
America Moves Forward, 51
An American ABC, 135
An American Plague, 21
Americans before Columbus, 58
America's Ethan Allen, 128
Amos Fortune, Free Man, 59
Anansi the Spider, 112
Anatole, 122
Anatole and the Cat, 121
. . . And Now Miguel, 56
Andy and the Lion, 137
The Angry Moon, 113
The Animal Family, 48
Animals of the Bible, 137

Annie and the Old One, 43
Anpao, 39
Ape in a Cape, 125
The Apple and the Arrow, 59
The Apprentice of Florence, 75
April's Kittens, 135
Arrow to the Sun, 110
Ashanti to Zulu, 108
Audubon, 72
The Avion My Uncle Flew, 64

Baboushka and the Three Kings, 119
Bambino the Clown, 130
Banner in the Sky, 56
Barkis, 137
Bartholomew and the Oobleck, 128
Bear Party, 126
The Bears on Hemlock Mountain, 57
Because of Winn-Dixie, 24
Belle Prater's Boy, 27
Belling the Tiger, 50
Ben's Trumpet, 107
Better Known as Johnny Appleseed, 60
Bhimsa, the Dancing Bear, 65
The Big Snow, 128
Big Tree, 63
The Big Tree of Bunlahy, 74
The Biggest Bear, 124
Bill Peet, 100
Birthdays of Freedom, Vol. I, 58
Black and White, 99
The Black Cauldron, 48
Black Fox of Lorne, 54
The Black Pearl, 46
The Blue Cat of Castle Town, 61
The Blue Sword, 36

Blue Willow, 68
Blueberries for Sal, 129
Boats on the River, 130
Book of Nursery and Mother Goose
  Rhymes, 123
Boy of the South Seas, 77
The Boy of the Three-Year Nap, 101
The Boy Who Was, 81
Boy with a Pack, 69
The Bremen-Town Musicians, 106
Bridge to Terabithia, 38
Bright Island, 71
The Bronze Bow, 50
Bud, Not Buddy, 24
By the Shores of Silver Lake, 69

Caddie Woodlawn, 73
Calico Bush, 77
Call It Courage, 68
Carry On, Mr. Bowditch, 55
Carver, 23
Casey at the Bat, 91
Castle, 108
The Cat Who Went to Heaven, 78
Cathedral, 111
Catherine, Called Birdy, 28
Cedric the Forester, 85
A Chair for My Mother, 105
Chanticleer and the Fox, 120
Charlotte's Web, 58
Children of the Soil, 76
A Child's Calendar, 92
A Child's Good Night Book, 133
The Christmas Anna Angel, 133
Chucaro, 52
Cinderella, or the Little Glass Slipper, 123
Clearing Weather, 81
Click, Clack, Moo, 92
Cock-a-Doodle-Doo, 136
The Codfish Musket, 72
Color Zoo, 100
Commodore Perry in the Land of the
  Shogun, 33
The Contest, 109
The Corn Grows Ripe, 55
A Corner of the Universe, 22

Courage of Sarah Noble, 56
The Cow-tail Switch, and Other West
  African Stories, 63
Crazy Lady, 28
The Cricket in Times Square, 51
Crispin: The Cross of Lead, 22
Crow Boy, 122

Daniel Boone, 69
The Dark Frigate, 83
The Dark Is Rising, 41
The Dark Star of Itzá, 79
The Dark-thirty, 29
Dash and Dart, 134
Daughter of the Mountain, 62
A Daughter of the Seine, 80
Davy Crockett, 74
A Day on Skates, 74
The Day We Saw the Sun Come Up, 118
Dear Mr. Henshaw, 34
The Defender, 59
The Desert Is Theirs, 110
Dicey's Song, 35
Dick Whittington and His Cat, 127
The Dinosaurs of Waterhouse Hawkins, 91
Dobry, 73
Doctor De Soto, 36
Dogsong, 33
Don't Let the Pigeon Drive the Bus, 89
The Door in the Wall, 60
Down Ryton Water, 68
Downright Dencey, 82
Dragon's Gate, 29
Dragonwings, 40
The Dream Coach, 83
Drummer Hoff, 115
Duffy and the Devil, 110
Duke Ellington, 93

The Ear, the Eye, and the Arm, 28
The Egg Tree, 126
The Egypt Game, 47
Eleanor Roosevelt, 29
Ella Enchanted, 25
Ella Sarah Gets Dressed, 89
The Emperor and the Kite, 115

Enchantress from the Stars, 44
Everything on a Waffle, 23

Fables, 106
The Fairy Circus, 77
The Faithful Friend, 96
The Family under the Bridge, 52
The Fearsome Inn, 46
Feather Mountain, 126
Figgs & Phantoms, 41
Finders Keepers, 125
A Fine White Dust, 33
Fish for Supper, 109
Fish in the Air, 129
Five Little Monkeys, 125
The Fledgling, 37
Floating Island, 79
Fly High, Fly Low, 121
Fog Magic, 66
The Fool of the World and the Flying
    Ship, 114
The Forest Pool, 136
The Forgotten Daughter, 75
Four and Twenty Blackbirds, 138
The Fox Went Out on a Chilly Night, 119
Frederick, 115
Free Fall, 101
Freight Train, 107
Frog and Toad Are Friends, 113
Frog and Toad Together, 42
Frog Went A-Courtin', 122
From the Mixed-Up Files of Mrs. Basil E.
    Frankweiler, 46
Frontier Living, 50
The Funny Little Woman, 111

The Gammage Cup, 52
Gandhi, Fighter without a Sword, 59
The Garden of Abdul Gasazi, 107
The Gardener, 94
Garram the Hunter, 78
A Gathering of Days, 38
Gay Neck, the Story of a Pigeon, 82
George Washington, 61
George Washington's World, 67
Getting Near to Baby, 24
Gillespie and the Guards, 121

Ginger Pye, 58
A Girl Named Disaster, 26
The Girl Who Loved Wild Horses, 107
The Giver, 28
The Glorious Flight, 104
Glory of the Seas, 75
Goggles!, 113
The Golden Basket, 72
The Golden Fleece and the Heroes Who
    Lived before Achilles, 84
The Golden Goblet, 50
The Golden Name Day, 55
Goldilocks and the Three Bears, 101
The Golem (McDermott), 109
Golem (Wisniewski), 94
Gone-Away Lake, 53
Good-Luck Horse, 133
The Good Master, 73
Grandfather's Journey, 97
The Graphic Alphabet, 95
Graven Images, 36
The Great Fire, 27
The Great Gilly Hopkins, 38
The Great Quest, 85
The Great Wheel, 53
Green Eyes, 124
The Grey King, 40
The Grey Lady and the Strawberry
    Snatcher, 106

Hansel and Gretel, 103
The Happy Day, 128
Harlem, 94
Hatchet, 32
Have You Seen My Duckling, 104
"Have You Seen Tom Thumb?", 67
Hawk, I'm Your Brother, 109
The Headless Cupid, 43
The Heavenly Tenants, 64
"Hello the Boat!", 70
Henry Fisherman, 128
The Hero and the Crown, 34
Hershel and the Hanukkah Goblins, 100
Hey, Al, 102
The Hidden Treasure of Glaston, 64
Hide and Seek Fog, 116
The High King, 45

Hildilid's Night, 112
Hitty, Her First Hundred Years, 79
Holes, 25
Homesick, 36
Hondo & Fabian, 90
Honk, the Moose, 73
Hoot, 22
Hope Was Here, 23
The Horsecatcher, 53
Hosie's Alphabet, 111
The House of Sixty Fathers, 54
The House of the Scorpion, 22
The House That Jack Built, 120
Houses from the Sea, 120
The Hundred Dresses, 66
The Hundred Penny Box, 40
Hurry Home, Candy, 57
Hush! A Thai Lullaby, 95

I, Juan de Pareja, 48
If All the Seas Were One Sea, 112
If I Ran the Zoo, 127
In My Mother's House, 135
In the Beginning, 31
In the Forest, 132
In the Night Kitchen, 113
In the Small, Small Pond, 97
Inch by Inch, 119
Incident at Hawk's Hill, 43
Indian Captive, 68
Invincible Louisa, 74
Island of the Blue Dolphins, 50
It Could Always Be Worse, 108
It's Like This, Cat, 49

Jacob Have I Loved, 37
Jambo Means Hello, 110
Jane's Island, 77
The Jazz Man, 47
Jennifer, Hecate, Macbeth, William
     McKinley, and Me, Elizabeth, 46
Joey Pigza Loses Control, 24
John Henry, 97
Johnny Tremain, 66
Joseph Had a Little Overcoat, 92
Journey Cake, Ho!, 124
Journey Outside, 45

Joyful Noise, 31
Juanita, 129
The Judge, 114
Julie of the Wolves, 42
Jumanji, 105
The Jumping-Off Place, 80
Just Me, 116
Justin Morgan Had a Horse, 64

Kildee House, 61
King Bidgood's in the Bathtub, 103
King of the Wind, 61
The King's Fifth, 47
Knee Knock Rise, 44

Leader by Destiny, 70
Li Lun, Lad of Courage, 63
The Light at Tern Rock, 59
Like Jake and Me, 34
Lily's Crossing, 26
Lincoln, 32
Lion, 121
Little Bear's Visit, 118
Little Blacknose, 80
The Little House, 134
The Little Island, 130
Little Lost Lamb, 131
Little Red Riding Hood, 104
Little Town on the Prairie, 68
Lon Po Po, 100
Lone Journey, 65
The Loner, 49
A Long Way from Chicago, 25
The Long Winter, 69

M. C. Higgins, the Great, 40
Madeline, 136
Madeline's Rescue, 123
Magic Maize, 57
Make Way for Ducklings, 134
The Man Who Walked between the
     Towers, 88
Maniac Magee, 30
Many Moons, 133
The Many Ways of Seeing, 45
Marshmallow, 134
Martin's Big Words, 91

The Matchlock Gun, 67
May I Bring a Friend, 116
McElligot's Pool, 130
Meggy MacIntosh, 78
Mei Li, 136
Men, Microscopes, and Living Things, 55
Men of Athens, 49
Mice Twice, 106
The Middle Moffat, 67
The Midwife's Apprentice, 27
The Mighty Hunter, 133
Millions of Cats, 81
Minn of the Mississippi, 59
Miracles on Maple Hill, 54
Mirandy and Brother Wind, 101
Mirette on the High Wire, 98
Miss Hickory, 63
Missing May, 29
Misty of Chincoteague, 63
Moccasin Trail, 58
Moja Means One, 112
The Moon Jumpers, 120
Moorchild, 26
"More, More, More," Said the Baby, 100
The Most Wonderful Doll in the World, 127
Mother Goose, 133
Mother Goose and Nursery Rhymes, 117
Mountain Born, 67
Mountains Are Free, 78
The Moved-Outers, 64
The Moves Make the Man, 34
Mr. Justice Holmes, 54
Mr. Penny's Race Horse, 122
Mr. Popper's Penguins, 70
Mr. Rabbit and the Lovely Present, 118
Mr. T. W. Anthony Woo, 126
Mrs. Frisby and the Rats of NIMH, 42
Mufaro's Beautiful Daughters, 102
My Brother Sam Is Dead, 40
My Father's Dragon, 62
My Friend Rabbit, 90
My Mother Is the Most Beautiful Woman
    in the World, 132
My Side of the Mountain, 51

Nansen, 68
New Found World, 65

New Land, 75
Nicholas, 83
Nine Days to Christmas, 119
Nino, 70
No, David!, 93
Noah's Ark, 90, 108
The Noonday Friends, 48
Nothing at All, 135
Nothing But the Truth, 30
Number the Stars, 31

Officer Buckle and Gloria, 95
Old Ramon, 51
The Old Tobacco Shop, 84
Old Yeller, 54
Olive's Ocean, 21
Olivia, 92
On Market Street, 105
On My Honor, 33
On the Banks of Plum Creek, 71
Once a Mouse, 118
One-Eyed Cat, 34
One Fine Day, 112
1 Is One, 122
One Morning in Maine, 125
One Wide River to Cross, 115
Onion John, 51
Ood-Le-Uk the Wanderer, 79
Our Eddie, 45
Our Only May Amelia, 25
Out of the Dust, 25
Out of the Flame, 77
Outside over There, 105
Owen, 98
Owl Moon, 102
Ox-Cart Man, 107

Paddle-to-the-Sea, 135
Pageant of Chinese History, 74
Pancakes-Paris, 62
The Paperboy, 95
Pecos Bill, 71
Pedro, the Angel of Olvera Street, 131
Penn, 70
Peppe the Lamplighter, 97
The Perilous Gard, 41
The Perilous Road, 53

Phebe Fairchild, 72
Philip Hall Likes Me, I Reckon Maybe, 41
Picture of Hollis Woods, 22
Pierre Pigeon, 134
The Pigtail of Ah Lee Ben Loo, 81
The Planet of Junior Brown, 43
Play with Me, 122
A Pocketful of Cricket, 116
The Polar Express, 103
Pop Corn and Ma Goodness, 114
Pran of Albania, 80
Prayer for a Child, 132
Puss in Boots, 100, 125

The Quaint and Curious Quest of Johnny
    Longfoot, 62
Queer Person, 78

Rabbit Hill, 65
The Railroad to Freedom, 76
Rain Drop Splash, 131
Rain Makes Applesauce, 117
Ramona and Her Father, 39
Ramona Quimby, Age 8, 37
Rapunzel, 94
Rascal, 49
Raven, 98
Red Sails to Capri, 58
The Relatives Came, 103
Rifles for Watie, 53
A Ring of Endless Light, 37
The Road from Home, 38
Roger and the Fox, 130
Roll of Thunder, Hear My Cry, 39
Roller Skates, 71
The Rooster Crows, 131
Rufus M., 66
Rumpelstiltskin, 102
Runaway Papoose, 81
Runner of the Mountain Tops, 69

Saint George and the Dragon, 103
Sam, Bangs & Moonshine, 115
Sarah, Plain and Tall, 33
Scorpions, 32
Seabird, 62
Seashore Story, 115

Secret of the Andes, 57
The Secret River, 55
Sector 7, 92
Seven Blind Mice, 99
Seven Simeons, 137
Shabanu, Daughter of the Wind, 31
Shadow, 104
Shadow of a Bull, 48
Shadrach, 57
Shen of the Sea, 82
Shiloh, 30
The Sign of the Beaver, 35
The Silver Pencil, 65
Sing Down the Moon, 44
Sing in Praise, 131
Sing Mother Goose, 132
The Singing Tree, 69
A Single Shard, 23
Skipper John's Cook, 126
The Slave Dancer, 41
Small Rain, 134
Smoky Night, 96
Smoky, the Cowhorse, 82
Snow, 93
Snow-White and the Seven Dwarfs
    (Burkert, illus.), 111
Snow White and the Seven Dwarfs (Gág,
    illus.), 137
Snowflake Bentley, 93
The Snowy Day, 118
So You Want to Be President, 91
A Solitary Blue, 35
Somewhere in the Darkness, 29
Song and Dance Man, 101
Song of Robin Hood, 130
Song of the Pines, 61
Song of the Swallows, 127
Sounder, 44
Spice and the Devil's Cave, 78
The Spider and the Fly, 90
Starry Messenger, 95
The Steadfast Tin Soldier, 124
The Stinky Cheese Man & Other Fairly
    Stupid Tales, 98
Stone Soup, 129
The Storm Book, 125
A Story A Story, 112

The Story of Appleby Capple, 60
The Story of Jumping Mouse, 103
The Story of Mankind, 84
Story of the Negro, 61
Strawberry Girl, 64
The Stray Dog, 91
Strega Nona, 110
A String in the Harp, 39
Sugaring Time, 35
Summer of the Swans, 44
The Sun Is a Golden Earring, 118
Surviving the Applewhites, 22
Swamp Angel, 96
Sweet Whispers, Brother Rush, 36
Swift Rivers, 76
Swimmy, 117
Swords of Steel, 75
Sylvester and the Magic Pebble, 113

T-Bone, the Baby Sitter, 127
The Tale of Despereaux, 20
Tales from Silver Lands, 83
The Talking Eggs, 101
The Tangle-Coated Horse and Other Tales, 80
Tar Beach, 99
Ten, Nine, Eight, 104
The Thanksgiving Story, 123
Theodore Roosevelt, Fighting Patriot, 57
There Was an Old Lady Who Swallowed a Fly, 94
These Happy Golden Years, 66
They Were Strong and Good, 135
The Thief, 26
Thimble Summer, 70
Thistle and Thyme, 49
Three Jovial Huntsmen, 111
The Three Pigs, 90
Thy Friend, Obadiah, 114
Tibet, 94
Time Flies, 97
Time of Wonder, 121
Timothy Turtle, 131
To Be a Slave, 45
Tod of the Fens, 81
Tom Paine, Freedom's Apostle, 53
Tom Tit Tot, 116
The Tombs of Atuan, 43

Tops & Bottoms, 96
The Treasure, 107
A Tree Is Nice, 121
Tree of Freedom, 60
Truce of the Wolf and Other Tales of Old Italy, 77
Truck, 106
The True Confessions of Charlotte Doyle, 30
The Trumpeter of Krakow, 80
Tuesday, 99
The Twenty-One Balloons, 62
26 Fairmount Avenue, 25
The Two Reds, 127

The Ugly Duckling, 93
Umbrella, 120
Up a Road Slowly, 47
Upon the Head of the Goat, 37
The Upstairs Room, 42

Vaino, 79
A Very Special House, 124
The View from Saturday, 26
The Village of Round and Square Houses, 102
A Visit to William Blake's Inn, 36, 106
Volcano, 33
The Voyagers, 83
The Voyages of Doctor Dolittle, 84

Walk Two Moons, 28
The Wanderer, 24
Waterless Mountain, 76
The Watsons Go to Birmingham—1963, 27
The Wave, 117
The Way to Start a Day, 108
Wee Gillis, 137
The Westing Game, 38
What Do You Do with a Tail like This?, 89
What Do You Say, Dear?, 120
What Hearts, 29
What Jamie Saw, 27
Wheel on the Chimney, 123
The Wheel on the School, 56
When Clay Sings, 111
When I Was Young in the Mountains, 105

When Shlemiel Went to Warsaw and
Other Stories, 46
When Sophie Gets Angry—Really, Really
Angry, 93
When Will the World Be Mine?, 124
Where the Buffaloes Begin, 105
Where the Wild Things Are, 117
The Whipping Boy, 32
Whistler's Van, 72
White Snow, Bright Snow, 129
The White Stag, 71
Why Mosquitoes Buzz in People's Ears,
109
Why the Sun and the Moon Live in the
Sky, 114
The Wild Birthday Cake, 128
The Windy Hill, 85
The Winged Girl of Knossos, 74
The Winter Room, 31
Winterbound, 72
The Wish Giver, 35

The Witch of Blackbird Pond, 52
The Witches of Worm, 42
The Wonder Smith and His Son, 82
Wonderful Year, 63
Working Cotton, 99
The Wright Brothers, 30
Wringer, 26
A Wrinkle in Time, 49

A Year down Yonder, 23
Yo! Yes, 98
Yolonda's Genius, 27
Yonie Wondernose, 132
You Can Write Chinese, 132
Young Fu of the Upper Yangtze, 76
Young Mac of Fort Vancouver, 68
Young Walter Scott, 73

Zin! Zin! Zin! a Violin, 96
Zlateh the Goat and Other Stories, 47